Mastering FORTH

Anita Anderson
Martin Tracy
MicroMotion

A BRADY BOOK
Published by Prentice Hall Press
New York, NY 10023

Mastering FORTH

A Brady Book
Published by Prentice Hall Press
A Division of Simon & Schuster, Inc.
Gulf + Western Building
One Gulf + Western Plaza
New York, NY 10023

Manufactured in the United States of America

2 3 4 5 6 7 8 9 10

Library of Congress Cataloging-in-Publications Data
Anderson, Anita.
Mastering FORTH.
Includes indexes.
1. FORTH (Computer program language) 1. Tracy, Martin, 1946–
II. Title. III. Mastering F.O.R.T.H.
QA76.73.F24A53 1984 001.64'24 84-14540

ISBN 0-89303-660-9

Publishing Director: David Culverwell
Acquisitions Editor: Terrell Anderson
Art Director/Cover: Don Sellers
Assistant Art Director: Bernard Vervin
Manufacturing Director: John A. Komsa

Typesetting: Micromotion, Los Angeles, CA
Printing: R.R. Donnelley and Sons, Harrisonburg, VA

Acknowledgments

We have many people to thank for their help on this project. Steve Tabor wrote the preliminary version of chapter 9, and Jennifer Brosious was responsible for all the illustrations and much of the design of the book. Coordination of public relations and marketing was handled by Linda Kahn. Mardi Rollow worked on paste-up and provided much appreciated moral support. Lyndell Martin assisted with the printing and patiently answered the phone. Some of the information we used was provided by the Forth Interest Group, Box 1105, San Carlos, CA 94070. We especially want to thank Henry Laxen, Michael Perry, and Kim Harris for their help with a language implementatoin model. And finally, we would like to thank Charles H. Moore, the father of FORTH, whose foresight we celebrate in this book.

Limits of Liability and Disclaimer of Warranty

Note to Authors

Contents

1 Introduction

FORTH is a high-level, stack-oriented language invented by Charles Moore in the early 1970s. Dr. Moore was looking for a simpler and more natural way to communicate with his "third generation" computer--hence the name FORTH (short for "fourth"-generation language). One of FORTH's first applications was to control the giant telescope at the Kitt Peak National Observatory and to analyze the data it collected. Since that time, FORTH has been used in a great many varied and complex projects such as:

a robot that uses tactile feedback to shear sheep

an automotive ignition analyzer

a peach sorter for a California cannery

an "expert system" for diagnosis of faults in diesel locomotives

a portable language translator

From the beginning FORTH has defied categorization; to begin with, it is designed for both systems programming and applications, and it is interpreted from the keyboard but compiled from mass storage screens. Programming consists of adding new commands to the small but powerful set of commands provided by the language; these commands now constitute both the program and actual additions to the language itself.

What makes FORTH so special?

- FORTH is extensible. Because you can add to the language, you can tailor it to your own needs. And since almost everything in FORTH is written in FORTH--the text editor, assembler, etc--you can access and alter all of it.

- FORTH is structured. Programming with FORTH encourages you to write logically complete, self-sufficient commands, built on existing commands, which are themselves used as the basis of more complex commands. This helps structure program design and simplifies and speeds debugging.

- FORTH is fast. FORTH runs much faster than many other high-level languages. Because the interpretation scheme is so elegant, interpreter overhead is minimal. Furthermore, FORTH includes a built-in assembler for speed-critical routines. As a result, FORTH can run almost as fast as machine code itself.

- FORTH is interactive. Each new word can be tested as it is defined, and changes can be made and checked on the spot.

- FORTH is powerful. It spans a power range from machine code to state-of-the-art structured and extensible languages. FORTH gives you direct access to the resources of your computer while providing you with sophisticated programming and data structures. It encourages you to write high-level programs by making it easy to optimize key sections of your code when you are done.

- FORTH is transportable. Only a small nucleus of code needs to be rewritten to move the entire language to a new computer. FORTH has been implemented on almost every computer developed to date.

- FORTH is compact. Its simplicity makes for an extremely compact language whose applications actually require less memory than equivalent machine-code programs.

- FORTH is not restrictive. You can extend it and experiment with it interactively. The time it takes you to master FORTH will be well spent when you find that your programs run faster, take up less space, do exactly what *you* want them to, take less time to debug, and provide the basis for more complex programs.

The FORTH-83 standard

FORTH's extensibility encourages you to form your own personal dialect of the language. At times, however, you may wish to write programs which run unchanged from computer to computer. To facilitate such transportability, the FORTH Standards Team was formed in the mid 1970s to select and recommend a common dialect of FORTH. Their work resulted in the FORTH-83 Standard, which was passed in August 1983.

In this book, we will introduce you to each of the commands required by the FORTH-83 Standard. In addition, we will be using many commands which, while not included in the standard dialect, can be written in the Standard and are therefore transportable. (We will provide you with the definitions for these words.) From time to time, we will also present extensions to FORTH which are not addressed by the Standard, such as strings and file manipulation. When we do, we will remind you that these extensions may differ from one standard system to another.

You will learn FORTH most effectively if you learn it while seated at your computer, because FORTH is designed to give you immediate feedback on your programs. We recommend that you try each example as you come to it and that you answer all of the exercises at the end of each chapter before going on to the next. (You will find answers to all the exercises at the back of the book.) And please feel free to alter and improve on any of the definitions we present. We hope that you find learning FORTH to be as enjoyable as it is rewarding.

2 Definitions

FORTH is an *interactive* language. It encourages you to try things out and responds immediately to your commands. To see how this works, start by pressing the <RETURN> key.

```
        <RETURN>  OK
```

FORTH says "OK." (In the examples in this book, we will always underline FORTH's response.) You didn't ask it to do anything, but FORTH responded anyway to tell you that it was listening. Regardless of your command, if it can be completed successfully you will see the OK when it's done--watch for it.

Commands are called "words" in FORTH. One of the simplest and most useful words is the one which prints a message on the screen. Look (don't type yet) as we define the word ALICE:

```
        : ALICE   ." CURIOUSER AND CURIOUSER!" ;
```

Certain components *always* appear in the definition of a word:

WORD	ACTION
:	The colon alerts FORTH that a definition is coming.
ALICE	Every word must have a name. Choose the name to reflect the word's purpose, as you will be asking for it later. Names can be as long as 31 characters. Use dashes instead of blanks to break up a long name, for example, A-LONG-NAME.
definition	In this case, the "definition" of ALICE is the message that you want to be printed, bounded by the "message markers" that tell FORTH where the

beginning and end of the message are-- ." (called "dot-quote") and " ("quote"). The ." must be separated from the message by a blank.

; The semicolon tells FORTH that the definition is over.

In painting, the empty space is just as important as the painted area--and in FORTH, the spaces are just as important as the words. All words must be separated by at least one space--otherwise FORTH wouldn't know where one word ended and another began. For clarity, always add two extra spaces between the name of the definition and the definition itself.

Now, type in the definition for ALICE (the shaded boxes are blanks). Don't forget to press <RETURN>:

```
: ALICE  ." CURIOUSER AND CURIOUSER!" ;  OK
```

Try out this new definition; type ALICE--and voila!

```
ALICE  CURIOUSER AND CURIOUSER!  OK
```

Of course the message that a word prints could be anything. To define a word that will print an asterisk, for example, follow the example of ALICE:

```
: STAR   ." *" ;  OK
```

Check to see that all the elements of a definition are in place: colon plus word name, definition, semicolon. Then try out the new word:

```
STAR  *  OK
```

Another word that is particularly useful is CR (called "carriage return"). Its function is simply to start a new line whenever it appears in your definition. Try defining a word (call it COLUMN) that will use STAR and CR to draw a vertical column of four asterisks:

```
: COLUMN <RETURN>
  CR STAR CR STAR   <RETURN>
  CR STAR CR STAR ; <RETURN>  OK
```

When you enter a long definition, you can break it into as many lines as you wish by pressing <RETURN> at the end of each line. FORTH won't answer OK until it sees the semicolon at the end of the definition.

Check the display your new word creates:

```
COLUMN
*
*
*
*  OK
```

The dictionary

All words--the ones already present in FORTH (like [:] and [;]), the ones you just defined, the ones you will define later--are stored in its "dictionary." Here is a summary of the words you have just used plus STAR and COLUMN, the words you just created. New words appear at the end of the dictionary.

WORD	ACTION
:	Enters a new definition into the dictionary. Used in the form: : <name> definition ;
;	Terminates a definition.
."	Puts a message into a definition. When the definition is later executed, the message is printed. Used in the form: ." message"
CR	Moves display "carriage" to the next line.
STAR	Prints an asterisk.
COLUMN	Prints a column of asterisks.

Much of the magic of FORTH is the ease with which it remembers (compiles) and carries out (executes) the definitions in the dictionary. When you type a new line and press <RETURN>, control is passed to a word called the "text interpreter." This interpreter reads the line word by word, from left to right, separating each word from its neighbors by the spaces between them.

```
  :      STAR     ." *"    ;
 word 1  word 2   word 3   word 4
```

As each word is found in the dictionary, its definition is executed. When all words have been executed, the text interpreter prints OK and waits for the next line.

If the word executed is [:] , a new definition is created in the dictionary; its name is given by the first word following the [:]--in this case, STAR. Subsequent words are then compiled into the definition until the word [;] is encountered. It is important to realize that no asterisk is printed when STAR is compiled. Learning to distinguish between when a word is created and when it is executed is one of the keys to understanding FORTH.

Modularity

Once you defined STAR, you were then able to immediately use it to create the more complex word COLUMN. STAR and COLUMN could then serve as "modules" in the construction of even more complex words. FORTH encourages modular programming by making it easy to create and name new definitions. Each new word can be immediately tested simply by typing its name. Enhance both efficiency and style with the following principle:

> **Words should do as little as possible. By keeping words simple, you can use them in more situations within many other definitions.**

Let's design some simple modules which, when combined with STAR, CR, and COLUMN, let you print giant letters made of asterisks. One way to group asterisks is to include them within the message markers. Define a word, for instance, that will start a new line and print five asterisks in a horizontal row--call it ROW:

```
: ROW   CR ." ***** " ;  OK
```

Does it behave the way you expected?

```
ROW
*****  OK
```

Now try a more complicated project: a word that will print a giant capital L. Do you see already how such a word can be defined using words you already have?

```
: L   COLUMN ROW ;  OK
```

At this time you may see the warning:

```
L ISN'T UNIQUE  OK
```

This is not an error; FORTH is simply telling you that the word L has already been defined. When this happens, FORTH will use the most recent definition--your definition--which is what you want it to do anyway.

Check to see if L works correctly:

```
L
*
*
*
*
*****  OK
```

What if you wanted to draw a capital T? There are several ways to do it. One way would involve first defining a word that would space over two blanks from the margin so that you could center the stem of the T. (Remember, whatever is inside the message markers is displayed on the screen as is--whether it's intelligible words, characters, or just blank spaces.) Call this new word INSET:

```
: INSET  ."  " ;  OK
```

When you combine INSET with STAR and CR, you can create STEM:

```
: STEM
  CR INSET STAR CR INSET STAR
  CR INSET STAR CR INSET STAR ;  OK
```

Check to see that STEM works:

```
STEM
  *
  *
  *
  *  OK
```

Now the T becomes easy--just combine ROW and STEM:

```
: T   ROW STEM ;  OK
```

And check the result:

```
T
*****
  *
  *
  *
  *  OK
```

In summary

The programs you will want to write will involve more complicated functions with more useful applications than drawing letters, but the principles remain the same.

> *Think modular*. By using FORTH words that are already available or that you have defined, you will be able to accomplish complex tasks in less time. It will also be easier to find your mistakes, since each word is labeled for easy reference and can be tested independently. Modular programming looks like a well-built pyramid, starting at the bottom level with words like STAR and CR and using them to build higher levels.

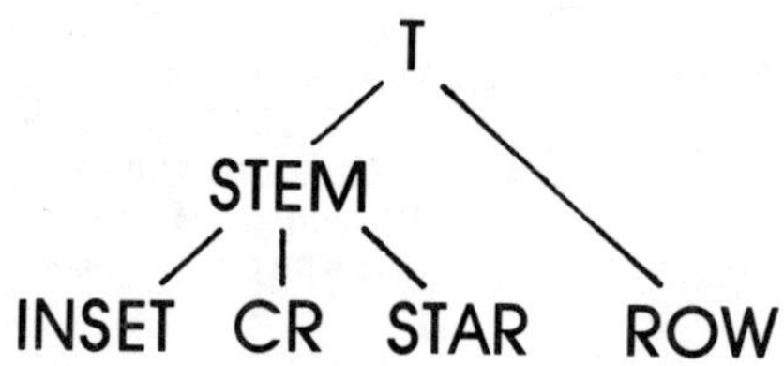

> *The word is the program*. There's no distinction between words and programs; STAR is a program, and so is T. All your FORTH programs will be combinations of previously defined words. That's why it's so important to understand definitions right at the beginning.

Exercises

Here are some simple exercises for you to try. You'll find the answers in the back of the book. Just remember, every [:] has a [;] , and every [."] has a ["].

1. Combine the actions of CR, INSET, and STAR into the new word BLIP, which will return, indent two spaces, and print one asterisk. Redefine T to use BLIP instead of STEM. Using only STAR, ROW, BLIP, and CR, make the new words "I," "C," and "E," respectively. Each letter should be no higher and no wider than five characters.

2. Define a word BOOP which, combined with ROW, lets you create the words H and U, which (guess what!) print the block-letters "H" and "U."

3. You have been asked to print a giant homecoming banner for Somewhere Technical High School. Using only words you have already written, create the word BANNER which, when executed, prints "HI-TECH" vertically on your terminal in large block-letters.

3 The stack

It would be quite impossible to build a dictionary large enough to hold a separate definition for every number. In fact, numbers are never found in the dictionary. What happens if you type 459 ? (We assume at this point you know to press <RETURN>, so we are not going to show it any more.)

```
459  OK
```

The text interpreter scans the input stream and finds the string of characters "459". It next searches the dictionary for a definition with the name "459". When the search fails, the text interpreter passes the string to an internal procedure called NUMBER, which attempts to convert it into a valid number. In this case, the conversion succeeds, and the number 459 results (to be continued below).

If the word you type is neither the name of a definition nor a number, the conversion in NUMBER fails, and the text interpreter assumes you've made an error. Execution stops, and the name is returned to you with a question mark. Try typing the nonsense word GORF:

```
GORF
GORF ?
```

If the conversion to a number succeeds, where does NUMBER leave the number? On the stack.

One way to imagine the FORTH stack is to think of a giant spring-loaded rack with numbers on it. Whenever a number is found in the input stream, NUMBER puts or "pushes" that number onto the stack. Try typing some numbers, separating them by spaces (and don't forget the <RETURN>):

```
1 2 3  OK
```

As each number is read and interpreted, it is pushed onto the stack, on top of any numbers already there.

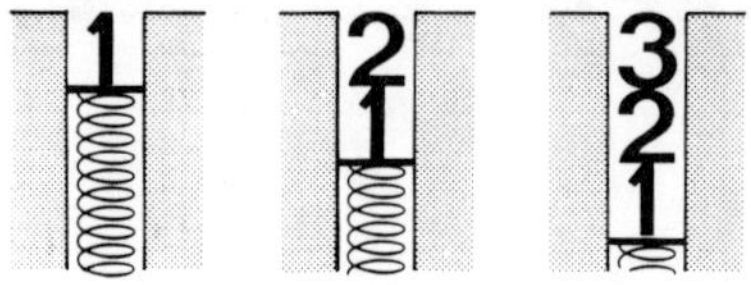

When you take the numbers off again (called "popping" them from the stack), their order is reversed. You cannot pop number 1 until you first pop numbers 3 and 2. This kind of a stack is sometimes called a LIFO or "Last In, First Out" stack.

You can use the word [.] ("dot") to pop a number from the stack and display it on your screen--try it:

```
. 3  OK
```

And then print the rest out too:

```
. . 2 1  OK
```

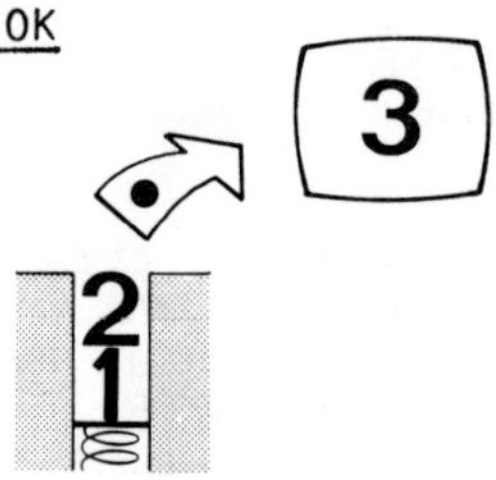

> The order in which these numbers are stacked is crucial to understanding FORTH. It is your responsibility to know the condition of the stack and the order of the numbers on it for accurate programming.

What happens if you type a [.] now?

```
. 0
. EMPTY STACK
```

The stack is empty and FORTH gives you an error message. (This condition is known as "stack underflow.")

Handy hints

You can use the word DEPTH to see how many numbers there are on the stack. The depth is zero when the stack is empty:

```
DEPTH . 0  OK
5 6 7  DEPTH . 3  OK
```

Use CLEAR to clear all the numbers from the stack:

```
CLEAR  OK
DEPTH . 0  OK
```

Addition

One of the unusual features of FORTH is the order in which numbers are entered for arithmetic operations. Instead of

```
3 + 4
```

as you might expect, FORTH uses

```
3 4 +
```

This idea, known as postfix notation or RPN (Reverse Polish Notation), makes sense when you think about FORTH's stack. It also makes complicated algebraic expressions easier to enter, as we will see later.

The word [+] ("plus") removes the top two numbers (also known as "arguments") from the stack, adds them together, and leaves the result on top of the stack.

Use [.] to see the result:

```
3 4 + . 7  OK
```

Now you can see why we need postfix notation; both numbers must be already on the stack before [+] can operate. To add a series of numbers, you can enter them this way:

```
5 13 + 1 + 14 + 25 + . 58  OK
```

or this way:

```
5 13 1 14 25 + + + + . 58  OK
```

Either way, [+] must find (at least) two numbers on the stack when it operates.

When a number appears inside a word definition, the compiler records the number for future use. The number won't be pushed onto the stack until the word is later executed.

```
: DOZEN  12 ;  OK
DEPTH . 0  OK
DOZEN . 12  OK
```

Subtraction

Postfix notation is used by all arithmetic operators, including subtraction:

```
        7 3 - . 4  OK
```

The operator [-] ("minus") needs blanks on both sides, just like any other word. Don't confuse this with the "minus-sign" which must immediately precede negative numbers:

```
        -7 3 + . -4  OK
```

Speaking of negative numbers, a useful word is NEGATE, which changes the sign of the top number on the stack:

```
        3 NEGATE . -3  OK
        DEPTH . 0  OK
```

A complementary word is ABS, which will give you the absolute value of any number:

```
        -3 ABS . 3  OK
         3 ABS . 3  OK
```

Consider the following definition:

```
    : -   NEGATE + ;
```

The word NEGATE reverses the sign of the number on top of the stack. The [+] operator will now give exactly the same results as [-] would have.

Multiplication and division

The word [*] ("star") pops the top two stack numbers, multiplies them together, and pushes the result back onto the stack:

```
        3 -4 * . -12  OK
```

Division is more complicated because it produces both a quotient and a remainder. The word [/] ("divide") will give you the quotient alone:

```
        15 6 / . 2  OK
```

The word MOD gives you the remainder alone:

```
15 6 MOD . 3  OK
```

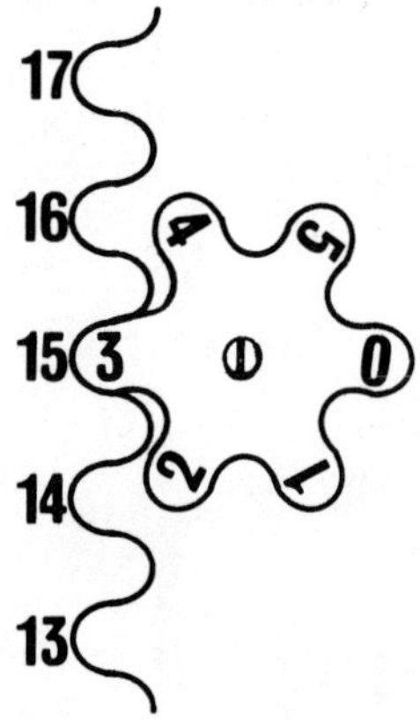

Note that 6 MOD will always return a number from zero to five. We will make use of this later in writing a random number generator.

The word /MOD ("divide-mod") combines these functions, leaving the quotient on top of the stack and the remainder underneath:

```
15 6 /MOD . . 2 3  OK
```

Division is "floored," meaning that if the result is negative and has a remainder, the quotient nearest to minus infinity (rather than nearest to zero) is returned:

```
-16 3 / . -6  OK
```

The remainder returned by MOD always has this property:

```
Numerator = (Quotient * Denominator) + Remainder
```

Check it out:

```
-16 3 MOD . 2  OK
-6 3 * 2 + . -16  OK
```

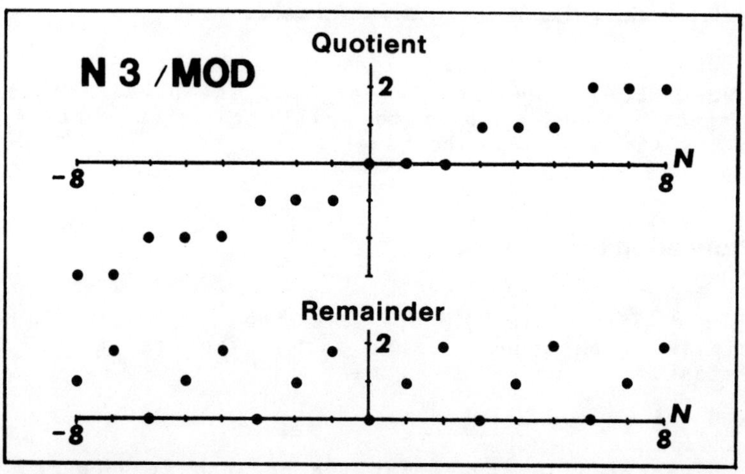

Division by zero is meaningless and the result is unpredictable.

MAX and MIN

The pair of words MAX and MIN are useful in limiting numbers to lie within a given range. As you may have guessed, MIN will give you the smaller of two numbers:

```
17 53 MIN . 17  OK
78 -22 MIN . -22  OK
```

while MAX gives you the larger of the two:

```
4 3000 MAX . 3000  OK
-8 -10 MAX . -8  OK
```

For example, you may wish to limit a thermostat control to the range between 62 and 75 degrees Fahrenheit. The expression 62 MAX 75 MIN will do this for you:

```
: COMFORT   62 MAX 75 MIN   ;  OK

55   COMFORT . 62   OK
65   COMFORT . 65   OK
90   COMFORT . 75   OK
```

Arithmetic expressions

One advantage of postfix notation is apparent when you try to work with complicated algebraic equations that have parentheses. With postfix notation, no parentheses are required. The following problem, for example:

$$\frac{4\,(3+2)}{(1+7)}$$

can be written in postfix notation like this:

```
3 2 + 4 * 1 7 + / . 2  OK
```

Let's walk through this example step by step, noting the stack contents at each point:

WORD	ACTION	STACK
3	Pushes 3 onto stack.	3
2	Pushes 2 onto stack.	3 2
+	Adds top two numbers.	5
4	Pushes 4 onto stack.	5 4
*	Multiplies top two numbers.	20
1	Pushes 1 onto stack.	20 1
7	Pushes 7 onto stack.	20 1 7
+	Adds top two numbers.	20 8
/	Divides top two numbers.	2

Outer limits

Ultimately, all numbers in a computer are represented by conveniently grouped "bits" of zeroes and ones. Numbers on the FORTH stack are 16 bits wide, so the arithmetic operators expect and produce 16-bit signed integers, also called "single-length signed numbers."

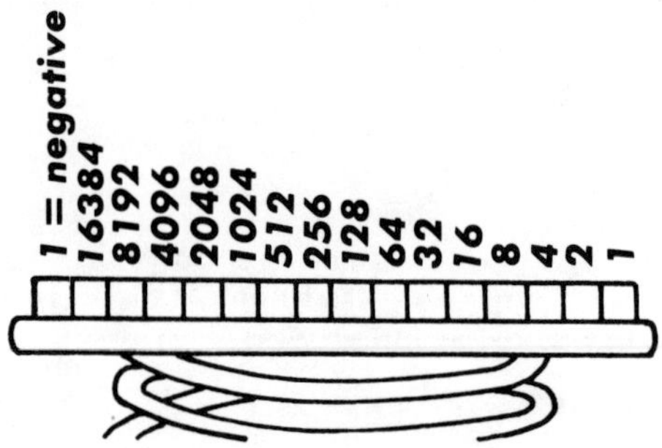

An integer is a "whole number," with no fractional parts. That's why 21 divided by 5 gives 4 instead of 4.2 or "four and one fifth."

Furthermore, 16-bit signed numbers are somewhat limited in size:

```
0000000000000000 is  0
0111111111111111 is +32,767

1111111111111111 is -1
1000000000000000 is -32,768
```

Adding 1 to the largest positive number gives you the largest negative number:

```
    32767 1 + .  -32768  OK
```

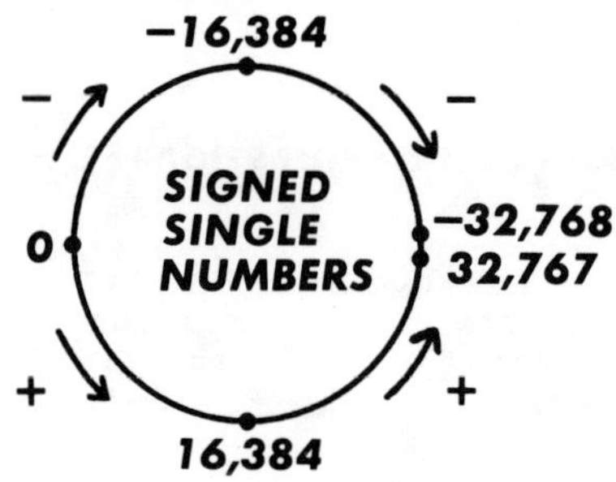

Other calculations can yield equally surprising results:

```
    20000 20000 + . -25536 OK
    20000     2 * . -25536 OK
```

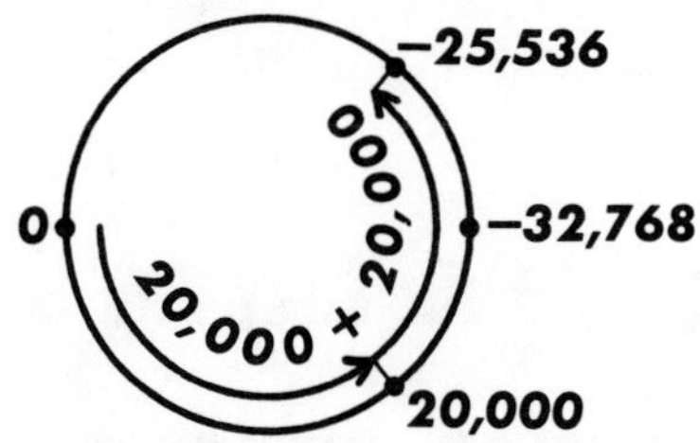

Fortunately, FORTH has ways of dealing both with extra-large integers ("double numbers") and with fractions, as we will see in later chapters.

Stack notation

The arguments required by each FORTH word and the result left on the stack after execution are so important that we use a special notation to keep track of them. The arguments required on the stack "before" execution are shown to the left of the dashed line and the results "after" execution are shown to the right (before --- after). Numbers on the stack appear in order of entry, so the number furthest to the right will be the top number of the stack. If no numbers are needed or produced, a blank is left on the chart.

Here are the definitions of the words we have used so far in this chapter:

WORD	STACK	ACTION
.	n ---	Prints number on top of stack.
+	n1 n2 --- n3	Adds two numbers, giving n3.
-	n1 n2 --- n3	Subtracts n2 from n1, giving n3.
*	n1 n2 --- n3	Multiplies two numbers, giving n3.
/	n1 n2 --- n3	Divides n1 by n2, giving quotient n3.
MOD	n1 n2 --- n3	Divides n1 by n2, giving remainder n3.
/MOD	n1 n2 --- n3 n4	Divides n1 by n2. n3 is the remainder and n4 is the quotient.
MIN	n1 n2 --- n3	Returns the smaller of n1 and n2.
MAX	n1 n2 --- n3	Returns the larger of n1 and n2.
NEGATE	n1 --- n2	Changes the sign of n1.
ABS	n1 --- n2	Gives the absolute value of n1.
DEPTH	--- n	Returns the number of items now on the stack.
CLEAR	---	Empties the stack.

And here are the words used in the previous chapter:

WORD	STACK	ACTION
: and ;	: <name> ... ;	Enters a new definition into the dictionary. (compiling word)
."	." xxx"	Compiles a message into a definition. When the definition is later executed, the message is printed. (compiling word)
CR	---	Moves display "carriage" to the next line.

Shortcuts

Certain common calculations have shortcuts in FORTH. These are words which are both faster and shorter than their alternative sequences; they should be substituted whenever possible. One such word is 1+ , which works like a 1 followed by a + :

```
13 1+ .  14 OK
```

The words 1- , 2- , 2* , and 2/ are analogous.

WORD	STACK	ACTION
1+	n1 --- n2	Adds 1 to n1.
2+	n1 --- n2	Adds 2 to n1.
1-	n1 --- n2	Subtracts 1 from n1.
2-	n1 --- n2	Subtracts 2 from n1.
2*	n1 --- n2	Multiplies n1 by 2.
2/	n1 --- n2	Divides n1 by 2.

Putting it all together

Now that you know how to define FORTH words and use basic arithmetic operators, you can begin thinking of ways to accomplish specific tasks. Here's a set of words, for example, that function together as a "change optimizer" program. They will take a random assortment of change and tell you how to present this amount with the smallest number of coins.

The first part of the program converts all the coins to their penny values so that they can be totaled.

```
: CHANGE      0 ;
: QUARTERS   25 * + ;
: DIMES      10 * + ;
: NICKELS     5 * + ;
: PENNIES         + ;
```

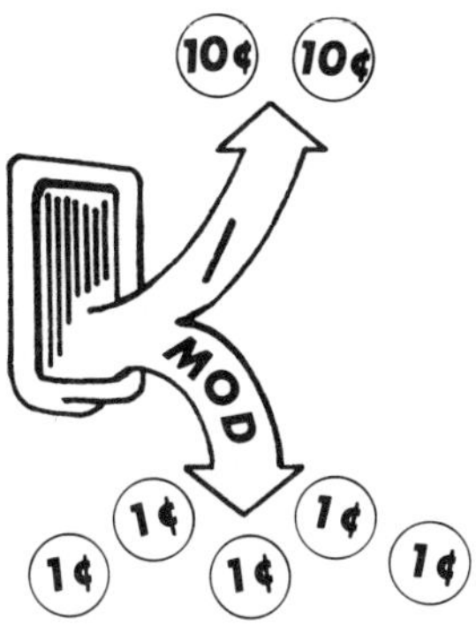

The first word, CHANGE, merely sets up the running total by putting a 0 on the stack. The word QUARTERS takes a number you provide, multiplies it by 25, adds it to the number on the stack (0), and leaves the result on the stack. DIMES and NICKELS multiply their respective numbers by 10 and 5 and add this to the total already on the stack.

PENNIES simply adds the number of loose pennies to the number on the stack. If the definition of PENNIES is simply [+], why have a word at all? Why not just use [+] in the program? Simply for readability.

Now your input can be expressed in this form:

```
CHANGE 3 QUARTERS 6 DIMES 10 NICKELS 112 PENNIES  OK
```

What's on the stack at this point? The sum of 3 * 25, 6 * 10, 10 * 5, and 112:

```
. 297 OK
```

The second part of the program redistributes the total starting with the largest denomination, quarters--so as to produce the smallest number of total coins. This is done with one word, INTO :

```
: INTO
  25 /MOD CR . ." QUARTERS"
  10 /MOD CR . ." DIMES"
  5  /MOD CR . ." NICKELS"
          CR . ." PENNIES" ;  OK
```

INTO divides the number on the stack first by 25; the quotient is printed on a new line followed by the message QUARTERS. The remainder stays on the stack to be divided by 10, and so forth. The final remainder represents the number of pennies left over; it is printed as is, followed by the message PENNIES.

When you use the program, the result looks like this:

```
CHANGE 3 QUARTERS 6 DIMES 10 NICKELS 112 PENNIES  OK
INTO
11 QUARTERS
2 DIMES
0 NICKELS
2 PENNIES OK
```

Exercises

1. The area of a triangle is given by the formula:

$$\frac{b * h}{2}$$

where b is the base of the triangle and h is its height (which is always perpendicular to the base).

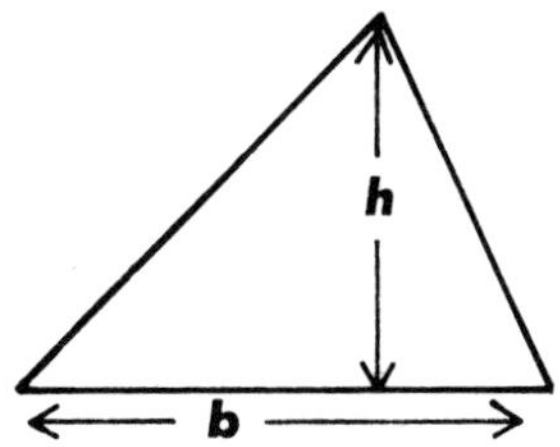

Define a word TRIANGLE which, given the base and height as arguments on the stack, computes and prints the area of the triangle. Since it's always a good idea to label your results, TRIANGLE should produce a result that looks something like this:

```
10 14 TRIANGLE
THE AREA IS 70  OK
```

2. Write a pair of words to convert temperature from centigrade to Fahrenheit and back again. The formula for this conversion is given below:

$$T_F = 32°F + \frac{9}{5} T_C$$

Choose names that will be easy to remember and use:

```
100 CENTIGRADE>FAHRENHEIT . 212  OK
 32 FAHRENHEIT>CENTIGRADE . 0  OK
```

3. After a busy day waiting tables, you notice that your tips include several strange coins. Modify the change machine to handle these coins. Their values, in pennies, are:

```
FRANCS  are worth  27 cents.
KRONOR  are worth  13 cents.
MARKS   are worth  40 cents.
TOKENS  are worth  75 cents.
```

The output of the change machine should look exactly like the one in this chapter. Write extra words to handle your new income and produce a result like the following:

```
CHANGE 4 QUARTERS 3 FRANCS 6 NICKELS 2 TOKENS INTO
14 QUARTERS
1 DIMES
0 NICKELS
1 PENNIES  OK
```

4 Stack manipulation

You will often need to alter the contents of the stack. You might want to make copies of certain numbers, delete others, move them around, or a combination of these. To make changes such as these, you can use FORTH's stack manipulation commands.

DUP

DUP ("dupe") takes the top number off the stack, makes a copy of it, and puts both numbers back on the stack.

Handy hints

You can use DUP to examine the top number on the stack without disturbing it:

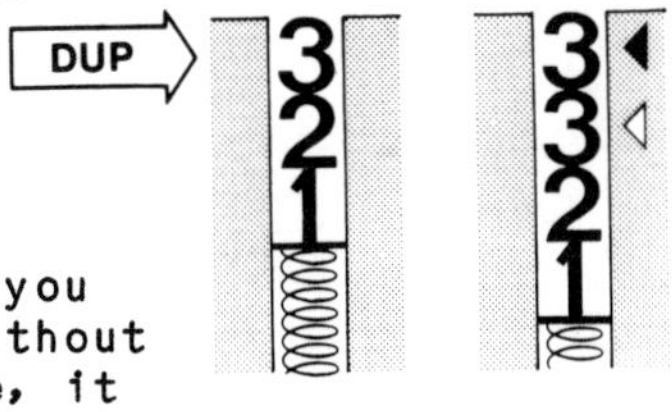


```
1 2 3  OK
DUP .  3 OK
. . .  3 2 1 OK
```

The word .S ("dot-S") lets you examine the entire stack without disturbing it. Furthermore, it displays the stack contents in the order they were entered--that is, with the top of the stack on the right:

```
5 7 9  OK
.S
STACK: 5 7 9 OK
. . . 9 7 5
.S
STACK: EMPTY OK
```

The word DOUBLE multiplies a number by two and prints the results. Because you want to print the number being multiplied as well as multiply it, you need DUP to make a copy:

```
: DOUBLE   ." TWICE " DUP . ." IS " 2* . ;  OK
4 DOUBLE  TWICE 4 IS 8  OK
```

DROP

DROP is the opposite of DUP; it takes the top number on the stack and discards it:

```
7 9 11  OK
DROP .  9 OK
DROP  OK
```

Here's a likely definition of MOD that would use DROP to get rid of the quotient and leave the remainder:

```
: MOD   /MOD DROP ;
```

SWAP

This word simply exchanges the top two items on the stack:

```
7 4 6  OK
DUP .  6 OK
SWAP .  4 OK
.S
7 6  OK
CLEAR  OK
```

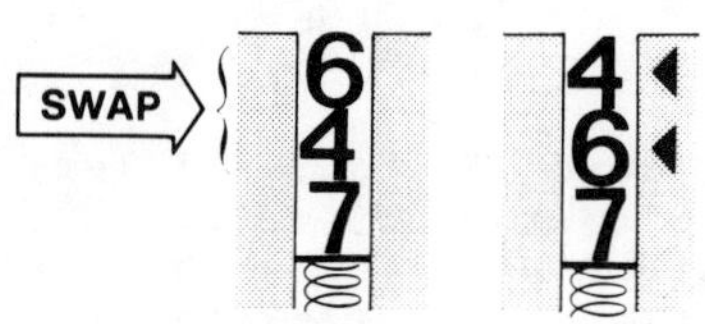

SWAP is especially useful whenever you have to deal with two numbers at once. In the following example, you need to keep track of how many events are completed and how many are still to be performed. Each computation must be performed at the top of the stack, so you need to SWAP the two numbers each time.

The word FINISH DROPs the number of incomplete events, since there is no point in printing this number and since it's a good idea to clear the stack before the next program.

```
: EVENTS  0 ;  OK

: TICK  1+ DUP . ." COMPLETED, "
  SWAP  1- DUP . ." TO GO "
  SWAP ;  OK

: FINISH  . ." COMPLETED. " DROP ; OK

10 EVENTS  OK

TICK  1 COMPLETED, 9 TO GO  OK
TICK  2 COMPLETED, 8 TO GO  OK
TICK  3 COMPLETED, 7 TO GO  OK

FINISH  3 COMPLETED.  OK
```

OVER

DUP copies the top item on the stack; OVER copies the item beneath it, leaving the copy on top of the stack. For example, suppose you want a copy of the top two items on the stack. Let's call the word that does this 2DUP ("two-dupe"). A good definition of 2DUP would be:

```
: 2DUP    OVER OVER ;
```

Why doesn't DUP DUP work the same way as 2DUP? Let's try some numbers and see:

```
1 2 3 DUP DUP .S
STACK: 1 2 3 3 3 OK
CLEAR  OK
1 2 3 2DUP .S
STACK: 1 2 3 2 3 OK
CLEAR  OK
```

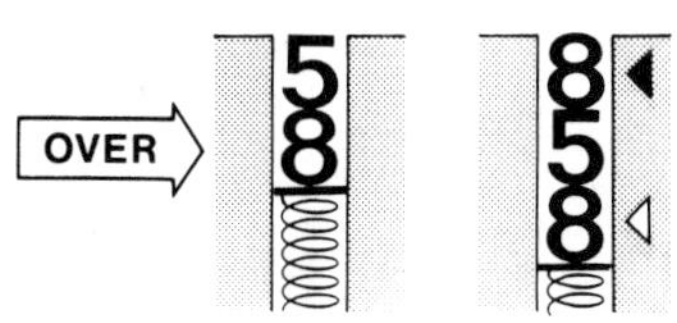

All DUP can do is make a copy of the number on top of the stack; you need OVER to get at numbers further down and make copies of them.

PICK

You can select or "pick" any item on the stack with PICK. As with OVER, the selected item is copied and the copy moved to the top of the stack. However, you must first push the "index" or number of the item you want on the stack. The top item has an index of zero, the second item has an index of one, and so on.

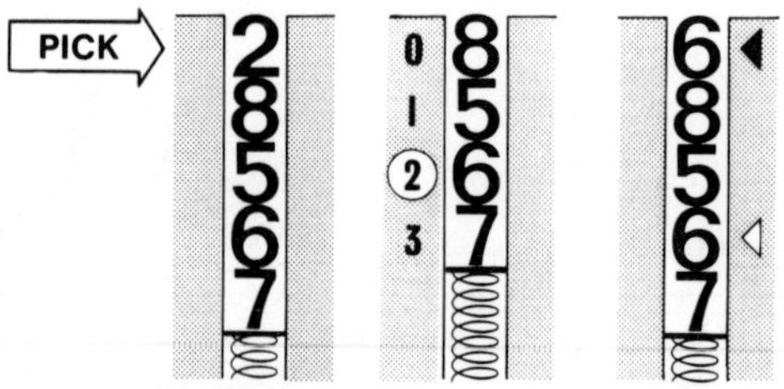

Suppose you would like to calculate the volume of a box. To do this, you need to multiply three items: the length, the width, and the height. You would like to print these measurements with appropriate labels before printing the volume. The word VOLUME uses PICK to accomplish this for you:

```
: VOLUME
  CR ." LENGTH: " 2 PICK .
  CR ." WIDTH : " 1 PICK .
  CR ." HEIGHT: " 0 PICK .
  CR ." VOLUME: " * * .  ;  OK

5 8 9 VOLUME
LENGTH: 5
WIDTH : 8
HEIGHT: 9
VOLUME: 360  OK
```

PICK is the most general stack copy command. We can define the other copy commands DUP and OVER by using PICK with the proper index:

```
: DUP    0 PICK ;

: OVER   1 PICK ;
```

But both DUP and OVER are usually much faster and produce less code than a corresponding PICK plus its argument does.

ROT

The commands DUP, DROP, SWAP, and OVER let you move or copy the top two items on the stack in any way you choose. Likewise, the command ROT ("rote") and its partner -ROT ("dash-rote") let you reach the third item on the stack. ROT moves the third item to the top of the stack. As with SWAP, the number is moved rather than copied. The second and top items are renumbered to become the new third and second items:

```
9 5 6 .S
STACK: 9 5 6  OK
ROT  .S
STACK: 5 6 9  OK
ROT  .S
STACK: 6 9 5  OK
ROT  .S
STACK: 9 5 6  OK
CLEAR  OK
```

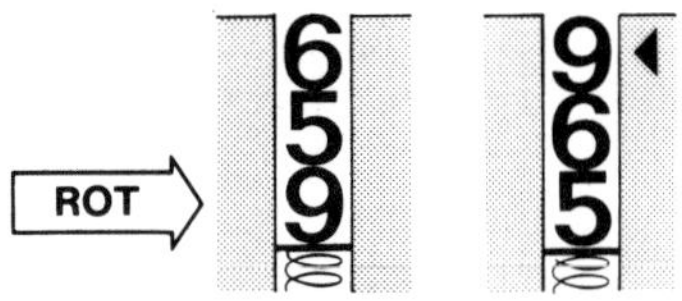

The command -ROT is the reverse of ROT. It moves the top item on the stack to the third position. Keeping the same numbers as in the last example, this is how -ROT would rearrange them:

```
9 5 6  -ROT .S
STACK: 6 9 5  OK
-ROT .S
STACK: 5 6 9  OK
CLEAR  OK
```

You can define -ROT thus:

```
: -ROT   ROT ROT ;
```

Suppose that three numbers on the stack represent three quantities and that you need to increment the third quantity by one. You could do this by alternating ROT and -ROT (that is, bringing the third number up to the top of the stack, incrementing it, and putting it back again):

```
9 5 6  ROT 1+ -ROT .S
STACK: 10 5 6  OK
CLEAR  OK
```

ROLL

ROLL takes ROT a step further; instead of moving just the third number on the stack to the top, ROLL will move any number you specify to the top, no matter how far down on the stack it is. Knowing what's on the stack, you simply indicate the index of the number you want moved to the top. ROLL takes the same kind of index argument as PICK; that is, the top item is numbered zero, the second item is numbered one, and so on.

```
3 5 8 9  2  ROLL .S
STACK: 3 8 9 5  OK
3  ROLL .S
STACK: 8 9 5 3  OK
CLEAR  OK
```

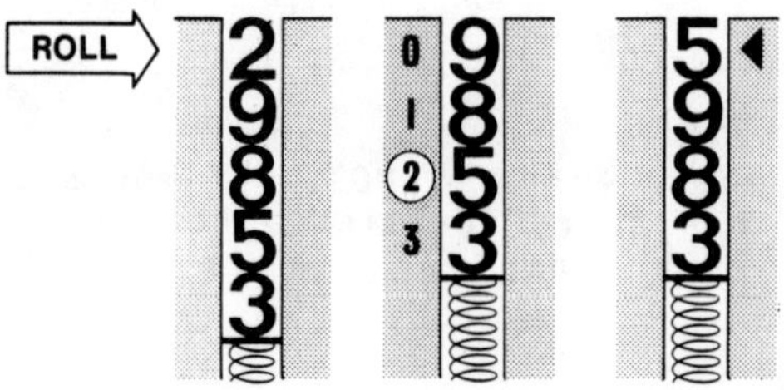

ROLL is the most general stack manipulation command. We can define the more specific commands SWAP and ROT by using ROLL with the proper index:

```
: SWAP   1 ROLL ;

: ROT    2 ROLL ;
```

The command 0 ROLL does nothing.

Here is a list of all the simple stack manipulation commands we've learned so far:

WORD	STACK	ACTION
DUP	n --- n n	Duplicates the top stack item.
.S	--	Prints, but does not destroy, all items on the stack, with the top item on the left.
DROP	n ---	Discards the top stack item.
CLEAR	--	Discards all items on the stack.
SWAP	n1 n2 --- n2 n1	Swaps the top two stack items.
OVER	n1 n2 --- n1 n2 n1	Copies the second item on the stack to the top of the stack.
PICK	... index --- ... n-index	Copies the index-numbered item to the top of the stack. The top item has an index of zero, the second item an index of one, and so on.
ROT	n1 n2 n3 --- n2 n3 n1	Moves the third item on the stack to the top of the stack.
-ROT	n1 n2 n3 --- n3 n1 n2	Moves the top item on the stack to become the third on the stack. The third item becomes the second and the second moves to the top.
ROLL	... index --- ...	Moves the index-numbered item to the top of the stack. The top item has an index of zero, the second item an index of one, and so on.

Double stack operators

Most of the simple stack operators you have learned have a "double" equivalent which operates on a pair of items at a time. We have already seen how 2DUP lets you duplicate a pair of items. Here is a list of the double operators, their arguments, and their results:

WORD	STACK	ACTION
2DUP	n1 n2 --- n1 n2 n1 n2	Duplicates the top pair of items.
2DROP	n1 n2 ---	Drops the top pair of items.
2SWAP	n1 n2 n3 n4 --- n3 n4 n1 n2	Swaps the top two pairs of items.
2OVER	n1 n2 n3 n4 --- n1 n2 n3 n4 n1 n2	Copies the second pair of items and moves them to the top of the stack.
2ROT	n1 n2 n3 n4 n5 n6 --- n3 n4 n5 n6 n1 n2	Moves the third pair of items to the top of the stack.

The double stack operators are especially useful when you are dealing with paired quantities such as fractions (which have a denominator and a numerator) and complex numbers (which have a real part and an imaginary part). You may have noticed that 2PICK and 2ROLL are missing from our list. That's because the stack seldom contains more than six items (or three pairs).

Putting it all together

The height of a falling object above the ground can be determined at any time (t) if its initial height (h0) and its initial downward velocity (v0) are both known. The height of the object is given by the formula

$$\text{height} = h0 - (v0*t) - 32t^2$$

where height is in feet and velocity is in feet per second. We can write a FORTH word which takes an initial height, initial velocity, and a time t (entered in that order) from the stack and leaves the final height of the object after t seconds.

```
: HEIGHT
  SWAP OVER *
  SWAP DUP * 32 *  + -  ;  OK
```

Let's take some numbers--say, an initial height of 1000 feet, an initial velocity of 100 feet per second, and a time of 3 seconds--and follow the computation:

WORD	STACK	ACTION
	1000 100 3	
SWAP	1000 3 100	SWAPs time and velocity.
OVER	1000 3 100 3	Copies and moves time.
*	1000 3 300	Multiplies velocity by time.
SWAP	1000 300 3	SWAPS product and time.
DUP	1000 300 3 3	DUPs time.
*	1000 300 9	Squares time.
32	1000 300 9 32	Adds 32 to the stack.
*	1000 300 288	Multiplies 32 by time squared.
+	1000 588	Adds product to velocity times time.
-	412	Subtracts sum from initial height.

Don't take our word for it, though--try out HEIGHT for yourself:

```
1000 100 3 HEIGHT  412  OK
```

We can do more with this problem, particularly to make the entry of the values clearer. In a case like this, it helps to "echo" the inputs by printing them on the screen properly labeled. The addition of a word that "surrounds" the original problem-solving word takes care of this need. It also can take care of exceptions--say, if the initial height was so low (or the velocity so high or the time too long) that the final height was less than 0, which wouldn't make sense. The 0 MAX in the following word, HEIGHT?, makes sure than no values less than 0 will be displayed.

```
: HEIGHT?
  CR ." INITIAL HEIGHT  : " 2 PICK .
  CR ." INITIAL VELOCITY: " OVER .
  CR ." HEIGHT AFTER " DUP .
     ." SECONDS:" HEIGHT 0 MAX . ;  OK
```

Now try the same values to see how much easier the result is to read:

```
1000 100 3 HEIGHT?
INITIAL HEIGHT  : 1000
INITIAL VELOCITY: 100
HEIGHT AFTER  3  SECONDS: 412  OK
```

And increase the time to 6 seconds to see that that the 0 MAX is doing its job:

```
1000 100 6 HEIGHT?
INITIAL HEIGHT  : 1000
INITIAL VELOCITY: 100
HEIGHT AFTER  6  SECONDS: 0  OK
```

Exercises

1. Using DUP, DROP, SWAP, OVER, PICK, ROT, -ROT, and ROLL, see if you can define the following stack operators:

3DUP	n1 n2 n3 -- n1 n2 n3 n1 n2 n3	Duplicates the top three stack items.
NIP	n1 n2 -- n2	Deletes the second stack item.
TUCK	n1 n2 -- n2 n1 n2	Duplicates and "tucks" the top stack item under the second item.

Can your definition for 3DUP be improved by using 2DUP, 2DROP, 2SWAP, 2OVER, or 2ROT?

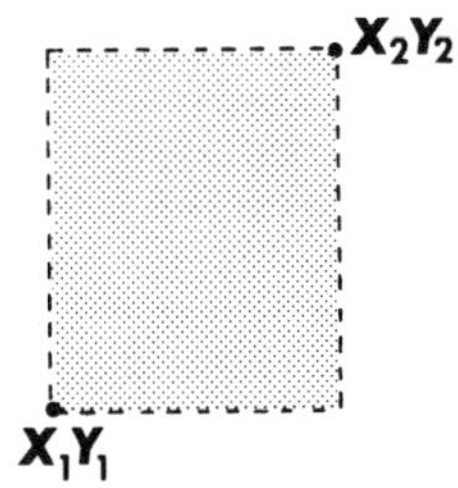

2. The area of a rectangle can be determined from the coordinates of either pair of opposite corners. Coordinates are usually given as a pair of numbers, with the horizontal coordinate given first.
If we call the coordinates of one corner X1 and Y1 and the coordinates of the other corner X2 and Y2, the area is calculated by this formula:

(X2 - X1) * (Y2 - Y1)

Define a word which expects all four coordinates on the stack and which returns an appropriately labeled result. Its stack notation will look like this:

RECTANGLE	x1 y1 x2 y2 --	Computes and prints the area of a rectangle, given the coordinates of two opposite corners.

It will work like this:

```
41 44 58 80 RECTANGLE
THE AREA IS 612  OK
```

5 The editor

Programming with FORTH is never a one-shot operation. Inevitably you will want to add or change something later as you think about your work a second time or devise a new purpose for your program. FORTH includes a separate program called the editor which makes it easy to both retain and improve upon existing words.

Words, words, words

All the words provided in FORTH as well as all the definitions you may add are compiled into the dictionary. You can use the command WORDS to examine the contents of the dictionary. First, add the following definitions:

```
: MARKER   ;  OK
: DANCE   ." CHARLESTON" ;   OK
: MUSIC   ." SWING" ;  OK
```

When you type WORDS, the name of each word in your dictionary will be listed on the screen, starting with the latest definition. To interrupt the listing, hit any key. To continue the listing, hit a key again; otherwise, hit <RETURN> to "abort" the listing:

```
WORDS
MUSIC
DANCE
MARKER
 ...
SAMPLE
 ...
FORTH-83
<hit any key>
<RETURN>  OK
```

(The contents of a dictionary change with each new definition added, so we have used "..." to indicate an arbitrary sequence of names.)

As you have seen, you can redefine words if you think of a newer or better definition, and FORTH will automatically use the latest version:

```
: DANCE   ." HUSTLE" ;
DANCE ISN'T UNIQUE  OK
: MUSIC   ." ROCK" ;
MUSIC ISN'T UNIQUE  OK

DANCE HUSTLE  OK
```

The new definitions are added to the dictionary, but the previous definitions are still there:

```
WORDS
MUSIC
DANCE
MUSIC
DANCE
MARKER
 ...
<RETURN>
<RETURN>  OK
```

To remove definitions from the dictionary, type FORGET, followed by the name of the word:

```
FORGET DANCE  OK
MUSIC SWING  OK
```

FORGET not only removed a definition (the latest DANCE), but also all the definitions which followed it (the latest MUSIC too). Your dictionary now looks like this:

```
WORDS
MUSIC
DANCE
MARKER
 ...
```

Try it again:

```
FORGET DANCE  OK
WORDS
MARKER
 ...
```

There is a limit to what you can FORGET:

```
FORGET DUP
FORGET PROTECTED
```

This is FORTH's way of saying that words below a certain critical point in the dictionary cannot be forgotten.

If you want to restore an erased word, you can type it in again and recompile it. But a long definition would mean a lot of retyping. When you create a FORTH word from the keyboard, the carefully typed lines that go into its definition are gone forever. There is no easy way to reconstruct the lines you typed (called the "source" code) from the word that is now part of the dictionary (called the compiled or "object" code). You need some way of saving what you type so that the words you create can be recreated as needed.

Files and screens

Fortunately, there is a way to save lines of source code--by typing them into computer "memory." We have already seen one kind of memory--the FORTH stack. The stack holds the arguments and "remembers" the results of the words you use. Another kind of memory holds the dictionary and remembers new definitions. These two types of memory are usually called "main" memory because they are immediately accessible to the computer.

Another kind of memory is called "mass storage," which is often cheaper and larger than main memory. Cassettes, floppy diskettes, and hard disks are examples of mass storage. It is the job of a program called the "operating system" to move information from mass storage to main memory and back again.

FORTH provides many of the functions of an operating system. It lets you type lines of source code to be saved in mass storage. You can then direct the text interpreter to read from mass storage rather than from the keyboard. The text interpreter treats the lines it finds there exactly as if you had typed them in again.

Mass storage is typically divided into a catalog and a number of files. A file simply holds an ordered collection of information, much like a file folder in a file cabinet. The catalog gives the name of each file and its location in mass storage.

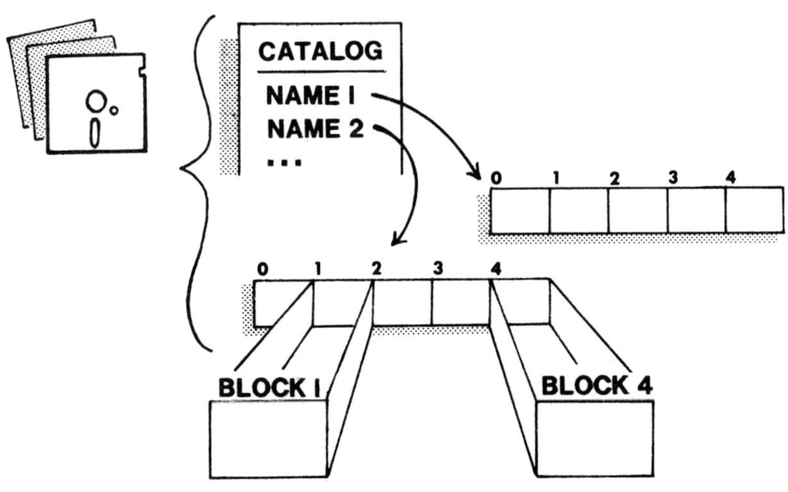

FORTH further divides each file into conveniently sized "blocks," which are moved in and out of main memory on request. The blocks are numbered sequentially, starting with zero. A block which is used to hold source text is called a "screen." Screens are divided into 16 lines of 64 characters each. This is more than enough for most definitions.

Selecting a file

The program which enables you to type source text into a screen is called the "editor." A well-designed editor lets you move, insert, and delete lines of source text. You can insert words within a line, search screens for a match with a given word, or replace one word with another. In short, the editor gives you control over the source text and encourages you to improve it.

Editors differ remarkably--some FORTH systems even give you a choice of editors. We will describe a general purpose "screen-oriented" editor that allows you to type text directly into a 16-line area on your console screen. We will further assume that you are using a floppy diskette or hard disk for mass storage and that you are somewhat familiar with the operating system of your computer.

Before using the editor, you must select a file to be edited. The files available to you are listed in a catalog and can be displayed with a command like CATALOG, DIR, or DIRECTORY--the same command you normally use with your operating system.

```
HOST OPERATING SYSTEM

   Files available:

     FORTH
     SAMPLE
     UTILITIES
     ...
```

The method of selecting a file also differs from one FORTH to another. We will discuss creating, selecting, and deleting files in great detail in a later chapter. The rest of this chapter assumes that you have a file called "SAMPLE" and a command, also called SAMPLE, that selects this file as the one to be edited. Type SAMPLE at this point:

```
SAMPLE  OK
```

You are now ready to examine and edit this sample file. All the commands taught in this section will work on any file once you know how to select it on your FORTH system.

LIST, LOAD and THRU

If you want to examine a screen, you can "list" its contents by typing the screen number, followed by the word LIST. See if there's anything on screen 1 of the sample file:

```
1 LIST

SCR# 1

 0
 1 : SIMPLE
 2   CR ." THIS IS EASY!"  ;
 3
 4
 5
 6
 7
 8
 9
10
11
12
13
14
15
OK
```

The word SIMPLE is not yet part of the dictionary:

```
SIMPLE
SIMPLE ?  OK
```

To redirect the text interpreter to read a screen instead of the keyboard (ie, to compile the screen,) simply type the screen number followed by the word LOAD:

```
1 LOAD  OK
```

Has SIMPLE been compiled?

```
SIMPLE
THIS IS EASY!  OK
```

Comments

Screen 2 of the sample file holds the source text of some

trickier words:

```
2 LIST

SCR# 2

 0 \ Somewhat trickier words.
 1 : TRICKY   ( start# -- end#)
 2 \ Starting equals ending number.
 3   3 +   ( add 3)
 4   2*    ( multiply by two)
 5   2-    ( subtract 2)
 6   2/    ( divide by two)
 7   2-    ( subtract two again)   ;
 8
 9 : TRICK2   ( start# -- end#)
10 \ The answer is always 3.
11   DUP  3 * 7 +
12   OVER + 5 + 4 /
13   SWAP -   ;
14
15
```

This screen shows how to use comments and indentation to make a definition easier to understand. Line 0 describes the contents of the screen in general terms. The \ "backslash" which begins the line is a FORTH word which causes the text interpreter to ignore all text to the right of the backslash for the rest of the line. Therefore, the text "Somewhat trickier words" is not compiled into the dictionary.

By convention, line 0 of each screen in a file describes the words on that screen. This makes it possible to quickly determine the contents of a file by reading line 0 of each screen. The line 0 comment often contains other useful information, such as the initials of the programmer who created the screen and the date the screen was last modified.

The next line reads:

```
1 : TRICKY   ( start# -- end#)
```

The word (("paren") is also used to add comments to source text. All text up to and including the next right paren is treated as a comment. The first line of source text for a definition should include a paren comment giving the stack notation for the definition (its arguments and results). Paren comments are also useful to explain the less obvious words within a definition. Comments should be used carefully, however, for these reasons:

- too many comments can make the definition difficult to read.
- comments about what a definition is supposed to be doing tend to be believed, *even if the code is incorrect*!

The word TRICKY is a good example of using too many comments. The comment "(subtract 2)," for example, doesn't really need to follow 2- .

> **Well-chosen names, indentations, and comments are the keys to writing easily readable definitions.**

The line numbers which appear on the left side of a listing are not part of the screen itself and are not seen by the text interpreter. You can see from the listing for screen 2 that the colon and opening comment for TRICKY and TRICK2 begin on the leftmost column of the screen, while the body of each definition is indented a few spaces. This allows FORTH utility programs to automatically build a simple glossary of your program. For example, a simple list of only those lines in screen 2 which begin in the leftmost column looks like this:

```
SCR# 2

 0 \ Somewhat trickier words.
 1 : TRICKY  ( start# -- end#)
 2 \ Starting equals ending number.
 9 : TRICK2  ( start# -- end#)
10 \ The answer is always 3.
```

Reformatting and sorting can make a simple glossary like this even more useful.

You can use 2 LOAD to compile screen 2 into the dictionary. You can also compile a range of screens with the command THRU. THRU needs the starting and ending screen numbers to compile:

```
FORGET SIMPLE  OK
1 2 THRU
..  OK

WORDS
TRICK2
TRICKY
SIMPLE
 ...

12 TRICK2 . 3 OK
```

As a courtesy, THRU prints a dot . for each screen it compiles so that you can gauge its progress.

One last remark about comments: screen 0 of a file cannot be read by the text interpreter--neither LOAD nor THRU can be used to compile it. Therefore, you can use screen 0 as a full screen of commentary on the words defined in the file and their use. You don't need any backslashes or parens either, because the screen is never compiled.

EDIT

The next screen in our SAMPLE file is empty:

SCR# 3

You will shortly be writing source text on this screen and editing it. Because you will be typing directly into the screen, you will need a set of non-printing keys to invoke the editing functions. On some computers you do this by pressing both the <CONTROL> key and a normal key at the same time. On other computers, you may have special editing or function keys marked with arrows, logos, or other symbols. We have assigned each editing function to a non-printing key of the same name. For example, <CRIGHT> means "non-printing key which moves the cursor to the right by one position."

We recommend that you fill out the following chart (or a copy of it) and that you keep it near your keyboard for easy reference for the rest of this chapter. The chart lists each editing function and the non-printing key which invokes it. To find the appropriate key on your keyboard, you may need to first refer to the documentation for the FORTH that you are using. Some FORTHs allow you to assign a key of your choice to each function. We recommend that you assign the same keys that you use for word processing.

COMMAND	KEY	DESCRIPTION
<CRIGHT>		move cursor to the right.
<CLEFT>		move cursor to the left.
<CUP>		move cursor upwards.
<CDOWN>		move cursor downwards.
<CORNER>		home cursor to upper left.
<FLIP>		show other side of screen.
<ENDLINE>		move cursor to end of line.
<TABRIGHT>		move right to next word.
<TABLEFT>		move left to previous word.
<TABUP>		vertical tab upwards.
<TABDOWN>		vertical tab downwards.
<INSERT>		insert a character at cursor.
<DELETE>		delete a character at cursor.
<WORDOUT>		delete a word at cursor.
<RUBOUT>		erase a character at cursor.
<SPLIT>		insert/split a line at cursor.
<JOIN>		delete/join a line at cursor.
<LINEPUSH>		push line onto the line stack.
<LINECOPY>		copy line onto the line stack.
<LINEPOP>		pop line from the line stack.
<FORWARD>		move forward one screen.
<BACKWARD>		move backward one screen.
<SAVE>		save screen to disk.
<COMMAND>		move to editor command line.
<DONE>		return to FORTH interpreter.
WIPE		erase current screen.
FRESH		restore screen if possible.
n MORE		request n more screens.
TOP		move to screen zero.
S string		search forward for string.
R string		replace match with string.

To edit screen 3, type:

```
3 EDIT
```

```



SCR#  3   0
```

You'll see the empty screen with the cursor in the upper lefthand corner (called the "home" position.) Take a look around your screen. It's not entirely empty--some identifying numbers appear at the bottom. The first number is the number of the screen, and the second is the number of the line the cursor is currently on.

Just for practice, type in these three lines, hitting <RETURN> at the end of each line:

```
This is line one.
This is line two.
And this is line three.
```

Press <CUP> twice to move the cursor up two positions to the beginning of line 2. Notice that the cursor travels right through the "A" in line 3 without changing it. You can move the cursor to the right without disturbing line two by pressing the <CRIGHT> key. Move to the second word (with five <CRIGHT>s):

```
This is line one.
This is line two.
And this is line three.
```

A more efficient way to move right is to use <TABRIGHT>, which puts the cursor at the beginning of the next word. Try two <TABRIGHT>s:

```
This is line two.

This is line two.
```

<TABLEFT> takes you to the beginning of the previous word:

```
This is line two.

This is line two.
```

<ENDLINE> takes you to the end of the current line:

```
          This is line two.
```

Pressing <ENDLINE> again takes you to the beginning of the current line:

```
          This is line two.
```

<ENDLINE> is an example of a "toggle" key, which means a key with two alternating functions. Press <ENDLINE> again to return to the end of line 2:

```
          This is line two.
```

Now move the cursor left with <CLEFT>, and type over the period with a comma:

```
          This is line two,
```

Move the cursor down to line 3 with <CDOWN>, and to the beginning of line 3 with two <ENDLINE>s. Type over the capital "A" with a small "a" and you will see:

```
          This is line one.
          This is line two,
          and this is line three.
```

<CORNER> toggles the cursor between home position and the beginning of the last non-blank line on the screen. Try it. <TABDOWN> moves the cursor five lines downwards, while <TABUP> moves it five lines upwards. If you try to move the cursor off the screen in either direction, it will simply stop at the edge. Try experimenting with all four cursor keys, all four tab keys, <ENDLINE>, and <CORNER> until you can confidently move wherever you wish on the screen.

Short screens

What happens if you type a longer line than your screen can display? (If your terminal can display all 64 characters of a line, type the following example in anyway--you will need it in the next section.) First, move down to the next available free line--try <CORNER> <CORNER> <RETURN>. Now type in the following long line, watching what happens on the screen:

```
    This is the beginning of an extremely long line.
```

As you approach the end of the line, the display suddenly changes:

```



an extremely long line.
```

Your display may differ slightly, depending on the number of characters per line (called the "width") of your terminal. What has happened?

Normally, the editor displays the "left side" of a 64-character-wide line. If your display is 40 characters wide, you would see the _first_ 40 characters of each line. When you move the cursor past the right side of the display by typing a long line or by repeatedly pressing <CRIGHT>, the editor switches to the "right side" of the line. With a 40-character-wide display, you would see the rightmost 40 characters of each line, starting with the 25th character. You can use <FLIP> to toggle between the left and right halves of the display whenever you choose. Try it.

Insert and delete

You can combine two lines with the <JOIN> key. Let's join line 2 to line 3. First, move the cursor to the end of line 2, then type a space:

```
This is line one.
This is line two,
and this is line three.
This is the beginning of an extremely lo
```

Now press <JOIN>:

```
This is line one.
This is line two, and this is line three
This is the beginning of an extremely lo
```

The two lines are joined at the cursor position. Lines can be split into two lines with <SPLIT>, which separates them at the cursor position. Try <SPLIT> to reverse what you've just done:

```
This is line one.
This is line two,
and this is line three.
This is the beginning of an extremely lo
```

Now we are right back where we started. If the cursor is in the middle of a line when <JOIN> is pressed, all characters to the right of the cursor, including the one under the cursor, are lost. Move the cursor to the beginning of "is" in line two and press <JOIN>:

```
This is line one.
This and this is line three.
This is the beginning of an extremely lo
```

This means that if the cursor is at the beginning of a line when you press <JOIN>, the entire line is deleted. Move to the beginning of line 2 and delete it:

```
This is line one.
This is the beginning of an extremely lo
```

Pressing <SPLIT> when the cursor is at the beginning of a line is equivalent to inserting a blank line. Try <SPLIT> and see:

```
This is line one.

This is the beginning of an extremely lo
```

Practice using <JOIN> and <SPLIT> on these remaining lines until you are confident in their use. Then home the cursor and delete all lines from screen 3 before reading on.

Character editing

Type the following definition into screen 3. With proper indentations and comments, it should look something like this:

```
\ Famous Quotes
: LAVOISIER  ( --)
\ 18th-century chemist.
  CR ." TO CALL FORTH A CONCEPT"
  CR ." A WORD IS NEEDED"
  CR ." --LAVOISIER" ;
```

Let's add some new materal--for example, Lavoisier's first name (Antoine). First, position the cursor over the L of his last name:

```
  CR ." --LAVOISIER" ;
```

Press <INSERT>. The message INSERT appears at the bottom of your screen to remind you that "insert mode" is now active. Now type in ANTOINE (and a space):

```
\ Famous Quotes
: LAVOISIER  ( --)
\ 18th-century chemist.
  CR ." TO CALL FORTH A CONCEPT"
  CR ." A WORD IS NEEDED"
  CR ." --ANTOINE LAVOISIER" ;



SCR# 3  0      INSERT
```

Notice how the characters to the right of the cursor are pushed over automatically to make room for your new material. If you insert too many characters, the end of the line may be pushed off the righthand edge of the screen. Some editors will prevent you from inserting more characters; others will warn you with an audible "beep." To leave insert mode, press the <INSERT> key again--it toggles you in and out of insert mode.

Now take out what you've just put in. You can do this several ways. You can use the <RUBOUT> key to delete the character to the left of the cursor, for example. Make sure the cursor is still over the "L" in LAVOISIER, then hit three <RUBOUT>s:

```
CR ." --ANTOI    LAVOISIER" ;
```

Although the cursor has moved three positions to the left, erasing as it goes, the remainder of the line didn't move at all. This leaves you with three blanks between names. You can delete one of the extra blanks, or any other character under the cursor, by using the <DELETE> key. Press <DELETE> three times:

```
CR ." --ANTOILAVOISIER" ;
```

The actions of erasing and moving the remainder of the line to the left can be combined by using <RUBOUT> while in the insert mode. Try typing <INSERT>, followed by five <RUBOUT>s:

```
CR ." --LAVOISIER" ;
```

The five letters to the left of the cursor ("ANTOI") have been deleted and the remainder of the line has moved left five positions. Choose the method of character deletion which seems the most comfortable to you.

There is one more delete key which deletes an entire word at a time. Since you are still in insert mode, retype ANTOINE, then reposition the cursor over the letter "A":

```
CR ." --ANTOINE LAVOISIER" ;
```

Now press <WORDOUT> to delete to the beginning of the next word:

```
CR ." --LAVOISIER" ;
```

Moving lines

The screen editor has a stack of its own--a line stack. You can push a line onto the stack with the <LINEPUSH> key and pop it back onto the screen with the <LINEPOP> key. Let's use the line stack to swap two lines on the screen. Move the cursor to anywhere within the first line of the quote:

```
CR ." TO CALL FORTH A CONCEPT"
CR ." A WORD IS NEEDED"
CR ." --LAVOISIER" ;
```

This line is now the "current line" because it is the line containing the cursor. Push the current line onto the line stack with the <LINEPUSH> key:

```
CR ." A WORD IS NEEDED"
CR ." --LAVOISIER" ;
```

The lines under the cursor move up to fill the gap. Now move the cursor down to the next line, making it the current line. Press <LINEPOP>:

```
CR ." A WORD IS NEEDED"
CR ." TO CALL FORTH A CONCEPT"
CR ." --LAVOISIER" ;
```

The lines at and below the cursor move down to make room.

To copy a line, use <LINECOPY>. <LINECOPY> works like <LINEPUSH>, except that it pushes a copy of the current line onto the line stack. Let's copy TRICK2 from screen 2 to screen 4. There are four parts to this copy operation:

1. Move to screen 2.
2. <LINECOPY> the lines of TRICK2 onto the line stack.
3. Move to screen 4.
4. <LINEPOP> the lines of TRICK2 from the line stack.

<BACKWARD> moves the editor back one screen (to screen 2). Press <BACKWARD> and move the cursor to the first line of TRICK2:

```
: TRICK2  ( start# -- end#)
\ The answer is always 3.
  DUP  3 * 7 +
  OVER + 5 + 4 /
  SWAP -  ;
```

Press <LINECOPY> five times. After each press, the cursor moves to the next line.

```
: TRICK2  ( start# -- end#)
\ The answer is always 3.
  DUP  3 * 7 +
  OVER + 5 + 4 /
  SWAP -  ;
```

Now use <FORWARD> to move to screen 4. Each time you hit <FORWARD> the editor moves forward one screen. Now that you are at the top of screen 4, which is currently empty, press <LINEPOP> five times. With each press, a line of TRICK2 appears on screen 4 until the definition is complete.

The command line

The screen editor has its own interpreter which allows you to execute any reasonable FORTH word without leaving the editor. Press <COMMAND> to use this interpreter:

```
: TRICK2  ( start# -- end#)
\ The answer is always 3.
  DUP  3 * 7 +
  OVER + 5 + 4 /
  SWAP -  ;



SCR#  4   5

ED:
```

The command line (preceded by "ED:") appears just below the screen number on the display. Try typing in a few FORTH commands, such as the following:

```
ED: 1 2 3 + .S 2DROP
STACK: 1 5  OK
ED:
```

The command line behaves exactly the same way as the normal FORTH keyboard interpreter, with three exceptions:

- Each line is preceded by "ED:" to remind you that you are still in the editor.
- Some special editing commands are available to you through the command line.
- Hitting <RETURN> after the "ED:" prompt exits the command line and returns you to the screen exactly where you left it.

Hitting <RETURN> lets you return to screen 4 (try it). But how do you leave the editor entirely and return to FORTH?

Finishing up

When you edit a screen, you are actually editing a copy of the screen which was moved from mass storage to main memory by the operating system. How and when the operating system rewrites the edited screens to mass storage varies from system to system.

When you press <SAVE> from within the editor, the operating system rewrites all the screens you have edited to mass storage. When you press <DONE>, you exit the editor and return to FORTH. The file you are editing is still active, and you may reedit any screen by typing in the screen number followed by EDIT.

At times, you may wish to leave the editor <u>without</u> rewriting the screens to mass storage. For example, you may have inadvertently deleted several important lines from a screen. If you have, exit the editor with <DONE> (don't press <SAVE> first) and then execute the FORTH command EMPTY-BUFFERS. This command deletes all screens from main memory. If you edit a screen now, a fresh copy will be read from mass storage. Unfortunately, if you have edited several screens, the operating system may have already rewritten some of them to mass storage.

The FORTH command SAVE-BUFFERS is identical to the editing key <SAVE>. Neither SAVE-BUFFERS nor <SAVE>, however, "closes" the file you are editing. Closing a file means rewriting all file changes to mass storage, updating the catalog, if necessary, and deactivating the file.

The command FLUSH closes all open files. You <u>must</u> use FLUSH

- before changing catalogs. If you are using floppy diskettes, for example, you must FLUSH before changing diskettes.

- after creating new files and before turning off power to main memory.

FLUSH includes a SAVE-BUFFERS command. If you type FLUSH now, the file SAMPLE will be closed and all your changes recorded in it. To "open" (activate) the file SAMPLE, use the command SAMPLE again. Assuming you are still editing screen 4, the command sequence to save all changes and return to screen 4 would be:

```
<DONE>
FLUSH  OK
SAMPLE  OK
4 EDIT
```

Editing shortcuts

You can use any reasonable FORTH words from the editor command line--you can even edit another screen. This lets you move text from one screen to another without having to use <BACKWARD> and <FORWARD> to pass through every screen between them. Let's copy the definition of TRICKY from screen 2 to screen 4. From the command line of screen 4, type:

```
ED:2 EDIT
```

You will be editing screen 2, just as if you had typed "2 EDIT" from FORTH. Use <LINECOPY> to push a copy of TRICKY onto the line stack. Now exit screen 2 with <DONE>. You will find yourself back on the editor command line. Return to screen 4 with <RETURN> and pop TRICKY onto the screen with <LINEPOP>.

Several handy editing commands can be used only from the editor command line. WIPE erases the entire screen you are currently editing. It is equivalent to deleting 16 lines but much easier to use. FRESH reads a fresh copy of the current screen from mass storage. Like EMPTY-BUFFERS, it lets you recover from editing mistakes.

Searching and replacing

To search the file for a a string and replace it with another string, use the commands "S" (search) and "R" (replace). Searching always takes place from the current cursor position on the current screen <u>forward</u> to the end of the file. To search the entire file, first move to screen 0 and home the cursor. This is easily done by using the word TOP from the editor command line.

```
ED:TOP
```

You will see the display change to screen 0. The cursor remains in the command line, but if you type <RETURN> you will see that it is actually in home position. From the command line, type S, followed by a blank, followed by the string you want to search for, followed by <RETURN>. For example, you can search the SAMPLE file for the word CR with the command sequence:

```
ED:S CR
```

```
: SIMPLE
  CR ." THIS IS EASY!"  ;
```

```
SCR#  1   2

ED:S CR
ED:
```

The display stops at screen 1 with the CR highlighted in some way--it may be extra bright, in inverse video, surrounded by brackets, or underlined. The cursor is still in the command line, but its active position is at the beginning of CR. Hit <RETURN> and see:

```
: SIMPLE
  CR ." THIS IS EASY!"  ;
```

```
SCR#  1   2
```

You can continue searching the file for the next occurrence of CR by returning to the command line with <COMMAND> and typing "S" again.

```
ED:S
```

```
\ Famous Quotes
: LAVOISIER  ( --)
\ 18th-century chemist.
  CR ." TO CALL FORTH A CONCEPT"
  CR ." A WORD IS NEEDED"
  CR ." --LAVOISIER" ;
```

```
SCR#  3   3
```

If you type the "S" command without a search string, it uses the last given search string again. In this example, each time you type "S," you will move to the next CR.

You will often need to replace several instances of one string with another. Suppose, for example, you decide to change the name of a word. You will need to search through the file for all occurrences of the old name, changing each to the new name. You can replace one string with another without leaving the command line by using the word "R." "R," like "S," is followed by a blank, the new string, and <RETURN>.

Let's replace each instance of CR in screen 3 with the string CRLF ("carriage return--line feed"). Since you have already found the first CR with the "S" command, simply type:

```
ED:R CRLF
```

```
\ Famous Quotes
: LAVOISIER  ( --)
\ 18th-century chemist.
  CRLF ." TO CALL FORTH A CONCEPT"
  CR ." A WORD IS NEEDED"
  CR ." --LAVOISIER" ;
```

"R," like "S," uses the last given string to make the replacement. To change the next CR to CRLF, type:

```
ED:S
ED:R
```

For practice, change the last CR to CRLF, then go back and change all the CRLFs to CRs again.

More screens

You will eventually fill all of the screens in your file with source text. When you do, your operating system may allow you to extend the file with the command MORE. From either the editor or the normal keyboard command line, type the number of extra screens you would like, followed by MORE:

```
2 MORE  OK
```

Once you have extended a file with MORE, you <u>must</u> FLUSH it before turning off power to main memory, or your extensions may be lost. Alternately, you can leave FORTH and return to the operating system with the command BYE. The definition of BYE includes a FLUSH command.

For practice, move to the last screen in SAMPLE using repeated <FORWARD>s. Type 1 MORE from the command line, return to the screen, and type <FORWARD> once more--this should move you to a new empty screen. Type in a line or two of your choice. Now return to FORTH with <DONE> and close SAMPLE with FLUSH. Reopen SAMPLE with the word SAMPLE and check to be sure that your new screen is still there.

WORD	STACK	ACTION
WORDS	--	Lists the words in the dictionary, starting with most recent.
FORGET	<name> --	Forgets <name> and all later words from the dictionary.
LIST	n --	Lists the contents of screen n.
LOAD	n --	Compiles the contents of screen n.
THRU	n1 n2 --	LOADs screens n1 through n2.
\	comment --	Treats the remainder of the current line as a comment.
(	comment) --	Treats the source text up to the next right paren as a comment.
EMPTY-BUFFERS	--	Erases the contents of all screens in main memory.
SAVE-BUFFERS	--	Rewrites all edited screens to mass storage.
FLUSH	--	Does a SAVE-BUFFERS and then closes all files.

Exercises

Retype the definitions you used in the exercises in Chapter 2 into screen 4 of the SAMPLE file--use as many screens as you wish. Be sure to use comments and indentations to make the definitions easy to understand. Use LOAD or THRU to compile these screens. Do the definitions work correctly? If not, FORGET them, correct the source screens, and try compiling them again.

6 Variables, constants and arrays

Computer memory comes in many types. One type of memory we have seen is the FORTH (LIFO) stack. It keeps a few top items handy but requires extra manipulation to reach items buried more deeply.

Another type of memory is called "random-access memory" (or just "RAM"). Each item in RAM is equally accessible and can be obtained in any order, which is what "random-access" means. This is possible because, unlike the stack, every location in RAM has a fixed numerical address. (Stack manipulation commands like PICK and ROLL use stack order numbers to identify items on the stack, but these numbers are only relative; RAM addresses, on the other hand, are permanent or "absolute.")

You can think of RAM as a long series of slots (or "cells") on a very large table.

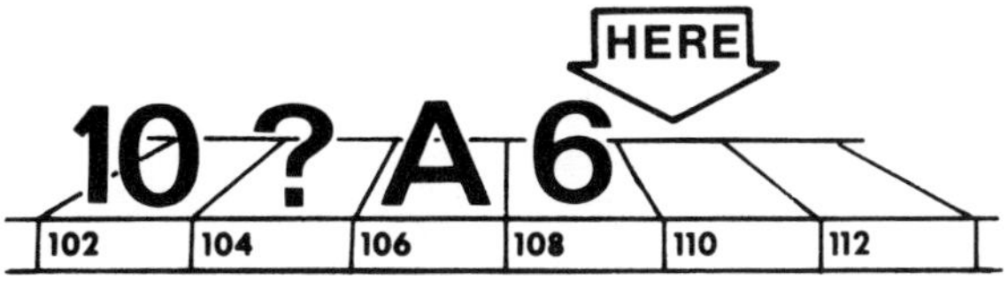

Each cell has an address--a number assigned to it by the computer according to its own internal system. Each cell also has a value in it. This value could be any number of things--the square root of 2, your checkbook balance, even the address of another cell!

> Be sure that you understand the difference between the address of a cell and that value stored at that address.

Since all addresses tend to look alike, FORTH lets you give some RAM cells names for easy reference and readability.

Variables

Some values change quite frequently--the number of inches of rain so far this season, for example, or the number of boxes of detergent in a supermarket's stock. When you want to use these values in your program without the hassle of manipulating them on the stack--and with the added convenience of referring to them by name--you should use a variable. Let's set up a variable that will have the name RAIN:

```
VARIABLE RAIN  OK
```

What exactly have you done?

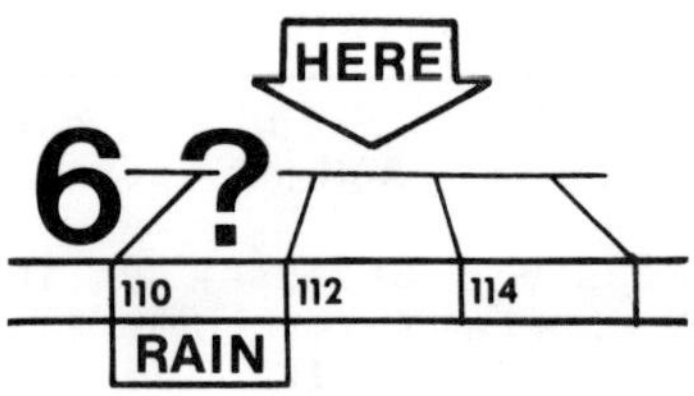

The interpreter creates a new dictionary word with the name RAIN. It then finds the address of the first available ("free") RAM cell. This is given by the word HERE:

```
HERE . 110  OK
```

(The number 110 is just an example of the number you might see at this point, which would also be considerably longer.)

The interpreter then assigns the name RAIN to this free cell and updates HERE to point to the next free cell. RAIN will now leave the address of its cell on the stack.

The interpreter then assigns the name RAIN to this free cell, and updates HERE to point to the next free cell. RAIN will now leave the address of its cell on the stack:

```
RAIN . 110  OK
```

BYTES

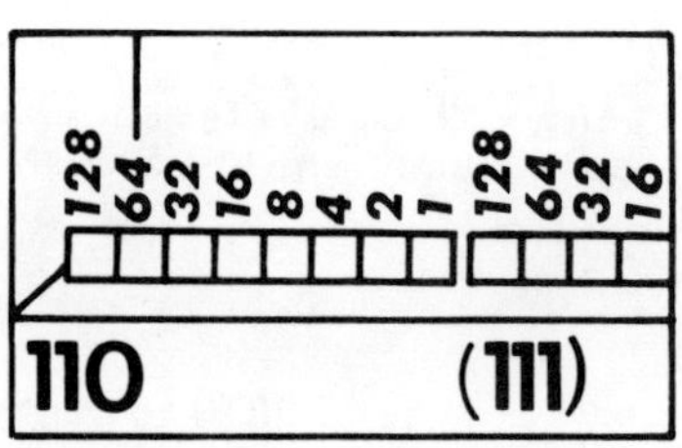

A "byte" in computer jargon means the smallest unit of memory that has its own address. On most computers, a byte contains 8 "bits" (zeroes or ones), and so has 1 of 256 different values (0 to 255). Since this range is too small for general use, bytes are often taken two at a time. That's why the FORTH stack and RAM cells are both 2 bytes wide.

In the example above, HERE has been advanced by 2 (bytes) to point to the next empty cell. You might reasonably expect HERE at this point to give 112. In fact, HERE will usually give a somewhat larger number. This is because the dictionary itself grows in RAM memory. When we add the variable RAIN to the dictionary, we add the four characters of its name and about 5 bytes of "overhead."

At this point the cell RAIN contains an unknown value. Let's "initialize" RAIN with a more useful number. Assume that there have been 12 inches of rain so far this season:

```
12 RAIN !  OK
```

The value 12 is placed on the stack and the address of the variable RAIN (110) is pushed on top of it. The operator ! ("store") then moves the 12 to the RAM location RAIN, replacing the unknown value that was previously there.

See if the value of RAIN is now really 12:

```
RAIN . 110  OK
```

You need the new word @ to get to the value of RAIN:

```
RAIN @ . 12  OK
```

The word @ takes an address from the stack (left there by RAIN) and copies the value it finds there back onto the stack. In other words, @ replaces an address with its value.

Note that you could get exactly the same result by using the address of RAIN, if you knew it. Ordinarily, however, you will never have to worry about the specific address of a variable; the name is all you need.

The process of bringing a value to the stack and printing it can be shortened with the word [?] ("question"), which combines [@] and [.] :

```
RAIN ? 12  OK
```

Changing the value of a variable is as simple as initializing it. Suppose it rained an inch yesterday, bringing the season's total to 13; you can store the new total just like you did the old one:

```
13 RAIN !  OK
```

You'll find that the old total has now been replaced:

```
RAIN ?  13  OK
```

An easier way to keep running totals is to let FORTH do the computation for you. Suppose yet another inch of rain fell; you could store this information as follows:

```
RAIN @ 1+ RAIN !  OK
```

Review the elements of this program to be sure that you understand them:

WORD	ACTION	STACK
RAIN	Puts address of RAIN on the stack.	address
@	Takes address off the stack, gets value from address, puts it on stack.	13
1+	Puts 1 on stack and adds it to value.	14
RAIN	Puts address of RAIN on stack again.	14 address
!	Removes both numbers, stores 14 at address.	---

And check to be sure that the total is correct:

```
RAIN ? 14  OK
```

Since adding to running totals is such a common operation, a special word, +! ("plus-store") will add the <u>second</u> number on the stack to the value stored at the address on <u>top</u> of the stack, saving you some steps. Try adding another 1 to RAIN this way:

```
1 RAIN +!  OK
RAIN ? 15  OK
```

It is also possible to add the value of one variable to that of another variable. You could set up a variable called TODAYSRAIN that keeps track of daily rainfall, for example, and then add that total to the running total stored in RAIN. If rainfall today was 2 inches, here's what you would do:

```
VARIABLE TODAYSRAIN  OK
2 TODAYSRAIN !  OK

TODAYSRAIN @ RAIN +!  OK
RAIN ? 17  OK
```

You can also include variables in definitions. Instead of adding a 1 to TODAYSRAIN every time an inch of rain falls, you can define a word that will take care of this for you--call it DRIP:

```
: DRIP   1 TODAYSRAIN +! ;  OK
```

TODAYSRAIN currently has a value of 2. Suppose it rains 3 inches today:

```
DRIP DRIP DRIP  OK
TODAYSRAIN ? 5  OK
```

A random example

Variables are useful whenever a named quantity has changing values. For example, one kind of random number generator generates a new random number by applying a formula to a previous random number:

```
new number = ([old number * b] + 1) mod m
```

This new random number in turn becomes the previous random number (the "seed") the next time around. We can use a variable called SEED to keep track of this number. Here is a simple random number generator RAND which uses SEED:

```
VARIABLE SEED  OK
1234 SEED !    OK

: RAND  ( -- new random number)
  SEED @  5421 *  1+  DUP SEED !  ;  OK
```

Check RAND against the formula. SEED @ gives us the previous random number, which we initialized to 1234. This is multiplied by 5421 (our "b") and is added to 1. The multiplication operator [*] limits the product to a 16-bit result, which is equivalent to performing a MOD of

65536 (our "m") on the result. Here is RAND in action:

```
RAND RAND RAND . . . -20463 -26032 4843  OK
```

We might also need to produce a more limited range of random numbers. We might want to pick a random card (only 52 choices) or throw dice (only 6 choices per die). We can limit the size of any number to a useful range with the MOD function. For example, any number MOD 52 gives a result from 0 to 51. We could include MOD within a new RANDOM, which is based on RAND:

```
: RANDOM  ( n --- random-number)
  RAND SWAP MOD  ;  OK
```

RANDOM will return a number from 0 to n-1. By adding 1 to whatever RANDOM returns, we get a number from 1 to n. If n is 6, we will get a number from 1 to 6, which is exactly what we need to model the throw of a die:

```
: DICE  ( -- die1 die2)
  6 RANDOM 1+  6 RANDOM 1+  ;  OK

DICE . . 2 3 OK
DICE . . 6 5 OK
```

Note: using MOD to limit the range of random numbers greatly reduces their randomness. This is because the digits on the right of a number produced by RAND are less random than the digits on the left. We will give you a better definition of RANDOM in a later chapter. If you wish to know more about random numbers and their generation, you might read Algorithms by Robert Sedgewick (Addison-Wesley, 1983).

Constants

Some values just never change--the number of days in a week, grams in a kilogram, etc. You can assign a name to any constant value with the word CONSTANT. Because you know the value of a constant when you first set it up, creating the constant and initializing it can be done in one step. Let's set up a constant to hold the number of days in a week, for example:

```
7 CONSTANT DAYS/WEEK  OK
```

And when you want to see the value or work with it, this is all you need to do:

```
DAYS/WEEK . 7  OK
```

Note that no @ is necessary; a constant puts its value on the stack, ready for you to use.

Constants are more than convenient and readable; they are also fast. If you define a constant to be the number 1, like this:

```
1 CONSTANT ONE  OK
ONE . 1  OK
```

using ONE is often _faster_ than putting a 1 on the stack!

A closer look

Before going on, it's worthwhile to examine in more detail how variables are really set up. When you type

```
VARIABLE <name>
```

two separate actions take place:

1) A new definition is created in the dictionary with the name <name> and instructions to push the address of the first free RAM cell (which often follows the definition) on the stack. This much is done internally with the word CREATE.

2) The first free cell of RAM is reserved for the variable <name>. The word HERE is updated to point to the next free cell, which normally follows the cell just reserved.
This much is done internally with the word ALLOT, which needs to know the number of free bytes to be reserved ("allotted").

Since a variable requires one free cell (which equals 2 free bytes), here is a possible definition of VARIABLE:

```
: VARIABLE   CREATE  2 ALLOT  ;
```

Any word which uses CREATE to make a new dictionary entry is called a "defining word." The defining words we have seen so far are [:] VARIABLE CONSTANT .

Arrays

A logical grouping of identically sized variables is called an array.

What are arrays good for? Mainly, convenience and space saving. The convenience comes in when you can refer to the whole group by one name, enhancing readability.

Arrays save space, too, by eliminating much of the computer "housekeeping" necessary to name each individual cell in an array.

What sorts of things would you want to group in an array? You might want to keep track of the calories you take in daily and add them up weekly, for instance. Instead of setting up seven variables, one for each day of the week and all in different memory locations, you can group the seven variables in an array and simplify the process of entering the values and keeping track of the totals.

The word VARIABLE is not what we want to set up arrays; as we've just seen, it allots only 2 bytes of memory space, which is only enough for one variable. But by splitting the action of VARIABLE into CREATE and ALLOT, you can ALLOT as many bytes as necessary to hold all the elements in your array.

To create the array CALS, first you need to make a new definition with the name CALS, and then you need to allot enough cells for 7 days' worth of calories, at one cell (2 bytes) per day:

```
CREATE CALS  14 ALLOT  OK
```

You now have a whole row of consecutive cells in memory, with the first cell named CALS.

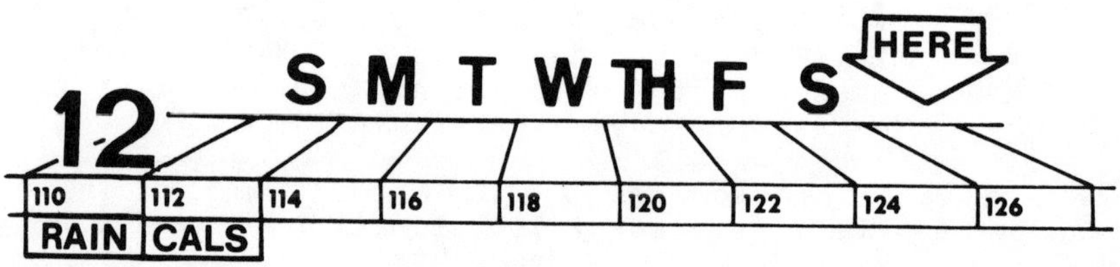

The action of CALS, like any new word defined by CREATE, is to leave the address of the first reserved cell which follows it on the stack. If you can find the address of the first cell, you can find the address of any cell by adding the appropriate offset, or distance between them. Since an offset is a difference between two memory addresses, it is given in bytes. Here's how it works:

Suppose your caloric intake on Sunday (the first day of the week) was 1200. Simply store that number at the beginning of CALS:

```
1200 CALS !  OK
```

On Monday you took in 2000 calories. All you need to do is increase the address of CALS by one cell (2 bytes) to store the 2000 in the right place:

```
2000 CALS 2+ !  OK
```

Rather than trying to remember the offset for each day (2 for Monday, 4 for Tuesday, 6 for Wednesday--which could get very difficult if you had a large number of offsets), use constants to name each offset and make it easier on yourself:

```
0 CONSTANT SUNDAY  OK
2 CONSTANT MONDAY  OK
4 CONSTANT TUESDAY  OK
6 CONSTANT WEDNESDAY  OK
8 CONSTANT THURSDAY  OK
10 CONSTANT FRIDAY  OK
12 CONSTANT SATURDAY  OK
```

Now when you want to store 1800 calories for Tuesday, this is all you need to do:

```
1800 CALS TUESDAY + !  OK
```

You can also set FORTH to the task of adding up each day's caloric intake so that all you have to do is enter each meal. Your Wednesday, say, starts with a 450-calorie breakfast:

```
450 CALS WEDNESDAY + !  OK
```

Later you eat a 600-calorie lunch:

```
600 CALS WEDNESDAY + +!  OK
```

The `+` adds the offset, and the `+!` adds the calories.

```
CALS WEDNESDAY + ? 1050  OK
```

This is tedious, isn't it--typing in WEDNESDAY + every time you want to enter another meal or check the total? By <u>factoring out</u> repetitive material such as WEDNESDAY + , you can simplify your input considerably. Several steps are necessary to do this, but they need to be entered only once--and you may be using your CALS array for a long time, long enough to appreciate the extra convenience.

First, set up a variable to hold the offset for the current day:

```
VARIABLE TODAY  OK
```

Second, a word to enhance readability; it will take the offset you give it and store it in TODAY:

```
: IS-TODAY   TODAY !  ;  OK
```

Third, a word to set the value of today's offset to 0, in case it still has the value from last week in it:

```
: WAKE-UP   0 CALS TODAY @ + !  ;  OK
```

Fourth, a word to store calories in the proper offset:

```
: MEAL   CALS TODAY @ + +! ;  OK
```

And fifth, a word to put the total on the stack so that you can display it:

```
: TODAYS-TOTAL   CALS TODAY @ + @  ;  OK
```

Now you can use the words in this sequence, plugging in caloric values such as these:

```
THURSDAY IS-TODAY  OK
WAKE-UP  OK
800 MEAL  OK
450 MEAL  OK
1000 MEAL  OK
TODAYS-TOTAL . 2250  OK
```

You may have noticed the repetition of CALS TODAY @ + in the preceding examples. Could this be factored out as well?

Tables

Arrays provide a good way to store tables and to access the information in them for computation or display. Entering each value in the table separately can be a chore if you have to take two steps to allot space and initialize the value. Fortunately, the word **,** ("comma") combines these two operations. It reserves one cell (2 bytes) and initializes it to whatever value is on top of the stack.

Let's make up a table to hold postal fees; then you can design a program that will take the number of ounces a package weighs, look up the proper fee in the table, and tell how much postage to put on your package. In our mythical postal system, the first 3 ounces cost 40 cents; 20 cents per ounce is added for the next 4 ounces; and 10 cents per ounce additional charge is made for the next 9 ounces, which brings the postage for one pound to $2.10 . The table has one entry for each ounce:

```
CREATE POSTAGE-TABLE
0   , 40  , 40  , 40  ,
60  , 80  , 100 , 120 ,
130 , 140 , 150 , 160 ,
170 , 180 , 190 , 200 , 210 ,
```

Now you need a word to "look up" values in the table. Call it OUNCES:

```
: OUNCES
  2* POSTAGE-TABLE + @
  CR . ." CENTS" ;  OK
```

When you type a number followed by OUNCES, FORTH knows to multiply the number by 2 (to get the offset), fetch the value at that offset, return the carriage, and print the value followed by the message "CENTS." See how it works:

```
5 OUNCES
80 CENTS  OK

6 OUNCES
100 CENTS  OK
```

Byte arrays

If the values to be stored in an array are small (from 0 to 255), you can save memory by storing them in an array of bytes rather than an array of cells. The operators ! , @ , and , have the "byte-sized" equivalents C! ("C-store"), C@ ("C-fetch"), and C, ("C-comma"). The "C" stands for "character" because a single printer character can be neatly stored in one byte of memory.

When you move a value from the stack to RAM memory with C! , the high-order byte is discarded. When you copy a byte value from RAM to the stack with C@ , the high-order byte is made zero. The order of bytes within a variable is undefined, so don't C@ from a variable unless you first C! into it.

We can rewrite the postage example to use an array of bytes. The table is built with C,

```
CREATE POSTAGE-TABLE
0   C, 40  C, 40  C, 40  C,
60  C, 80  C, 100 C, 120 C,
130 C, 140 C, 150 C, 160 C,
170 C, 180 C, 190 C, 200 C, 210 C,
```

and the new definition for OUNCES is

```
: OUNCES
  POSTAGE-TABLE + C@
  CR . ." CENTS" ;  OK
```

Check to see that it produces the same results:

```
5 OUNCES
80 CENTS  OK
```

WORD	STACK	ACTION
VARIABLE <name>	--- --- addr	Creates a one-cell (2-byte) variable named <name>. When <name> is executed, it will push the address of this cell on the stack.
!	n addr ---	Stores the value n at the address addr.
@	addr --- n	Copies the value n from address addr to the stack.
?	addr ---	Prints the value n stored at address addr.
+!	n addr ---	Adds n to the value found at address addr.
CONSTANT <name>	n --- --- n	Creates a constant named <name> with a value of n. When <name> is executed, the value n will be pushed onto the stack.
CREATE <name>	--- --- addr	Creates a dictionary entry named <name>. When executed, <name> will push the address of the first memory cell which follows the word <name> onto the stack. No memory is actually reserved by CREATE.
HERE	--- addr	Leaves address of next free byte in the dictionary.
ALLOT	n-bytes ---	Reserves n bytes of RAM memory. ALLOT usually follows a defining word.
,	n ---	Reserves one cell (2 bytes) of memory, initializing it to the value n.
C!	8b addr ---	Stores the low-order byte of 8b at address addr.
C@	addr --- 8b	Copies the byte 8b from address addr to the stack.
C,	8b ---	Reserves one byte of memory, initializing it to the value 8b.

Double variables and constants

Paired quantities such as spatial coordinates or complex numbers can be stored in and retrieved from special double-sized variables and constants.

Use 2VARIABLE and 2CONSTANT to build the named 4-byte quantities. Use 2@ and 2! to move the paired quantities to and from the stack:

```
12 20 2CONSTANT BOTH  OK
BOTH .S
STACK: 12 20  OK
CLEAR  OK

2VARIABLE HIS-AND-HERS  OK
1 10 HIS-AND-HERS 2!  OK
HIS-AND-HERS 2@ .S
STACK: 1 10  OK
CLEAR  OK
```

The high-order item of the pair, that is, the one closest to the top of the stack, is stored in the first 2 bytes of the 2VARIABLE:

```
HIS-AND-HERS @ .  10  OK
```

WORD	STACK	ACTION
2VARIABLE <name>	---	Creates a 2-cell (4-byte) variable named <name>.
	--- addr	When <name> is executed, it will push the address of the first cell onto the stack.
2CONSTANT <name>	n ---	Creates a double constant named <name> with the value pair n1 and n2.
	--- n	When <name> is executed, this pair will be pushed onto the stack.
2!	n1 n2 addr ---	Stores the pair n1 and n2 at the address addr.
2@	addr --- n1 n2	Copies the pair n1 and n2 from address addr to the stack.

Exercises

1. Write the words OFF and ON which set variables to false (0) and true (-1), respectively:

```
VARIABLE SWITCH  OK

SWITCH OFF  OK
SWITCH ? 0  OK
SWITCH ON  OK
SWITCH ? -1  OK
```

2. The FORTH Interest Group (FIG) uses a form of VARIABLE which takes its initial value from the stack. Write a defining word FIG-VARIABLE which creates FIG-FORTH variables:

```
4 FIG-VARIABLE X  OK
X ? 4  OK
```

3. You will often find that an extra stack is just what you need to solve a problem. Try creating your own stack with an array called STACK and the words PUSH and POP. PUSH and POP should work like this:

```
3 PUSH  OK
4 PUSH  OK

POP . 4  OK
POP . 3  OK
```

   You'll need an additional variable to keep track of the next available stack position.

   PUSH should do something reasonable even if your STACK is full. (Hint: use MAX and MIN.) What might POP do with an empty stack?

7 Flow of control

Often you will come to a point in your program where a decision needs to be made--that is, if the temperature of a room is over 85 degrees, turn the air conditioner on. Or suppose you are programming a dice game like "craps." The first time you roll the dice, you need to see if their total equals 12 or 2; if it does, you lose, and if it doesn't, you can continue playing.

The decision-making process can always be divided into two parts: first, information about a circumstance or "condition" on which the decision depends (in the case of craps, whether the total equals 12 or 2); and second, what the possible responses will be (to end the game, to reroll, etc).

Every time FORTH checks for a condition, it expects to find a number on the stack with one of two values--true or false--called a "Boolean flag." True is represented by -1, false by 0. These flags are left on the stack by words called "logical operators" and are used to decide between alternative courses of action. For example, the following words compare two numbers to each other and leave a true/false condition on the stack, depending on what they find:

WORD	STACK	ACTION
=	n1 n2 --- flag	"Equal" returns true (-1) if n1 equals n2.
<>	n1 n2 --- flag	"Unequal" returns true if n1 and n2 are unequal.
>	n1 n2 --- flag	"Greater-than" returns true if n1 is greater than n2.
<	n1 n2 --- flag	"Less-than" returns true if n1 is less than n2.

Here are the comparison operators in action:

```
11 12 =   .   0  OK
12 12 =   .  -1  OK
12 12 <>  .   0  OK

6  5  >   .  -1  OK
11 6  <   .   0  OK
-6 6  <   .  -1  OK
```

Though at this point it is necessary to print the flags to see how the logical operators work, remember that you will usually leave them on the stack to be passed on to the next part of the program.

Another group of logical operators compares a single number on the stack to zero:

WORD	STACK	ACTION
0=	n --- flag	"Zero-equals" returns true if n equals 0.
0<>	n --- flag	"Zero-unequals" returns true if n is unequal to 0.
0>	n --- flag	"Zero-greater-than" returns true if n is greater than 0.
0<	n --- flag	"Zero-less-than" returns true if n is negative.

```
5  0= . 0  OK
0  0= . -1  OK
5  0> . -1  OK
-5 0< . -1  OK
5  0< . 0 OK
```

The operator 0= can be used to reverse the value of a flag:

```
0  0= . -1  OK
-1 0= . 0  OK
```

AND, OR, and NOT

The logical operators AND, OR, and NOT allow you to make more sophisticated decisions based on conditions returned by the other logical operators.

AND returns true only if the top *and* second flags on the stack are true. OR returns true if either the top *or* second flag (or both) is true:

```
0 5 <  5 8 < AND .  -1  OK
0 9 <  9 8 < AND .   0  OK

3 3 =  3 4 =  OR .  -1  OK
3 5 =  3 6 =  OR .   0  OK
```

NOT, like 0=, *reverses* the top flag on the stack:

```
5 5 = NOT .  0  OK
5 6 > NOT . -1  OK
```

We will show you later how to use AND, OR, and NOT to manipulate non-Boolean values. Meanwhile, be sure when you form a logical expression (combination of conditions) that at least one of the arguments to AND, OR, and NOT is a Boolean flag. You can use 0<> to make sure that this is the case.

Let's suppose your computer has a built-in clock which you've used to store the current month (a number from 1 to 12) and current year (a four-digit number like 1984) into the variables MONTH and YEAR. Now suppose you would like to write a word called DAYS which returns the number of days in the current month. One approach you could take would be to create a table of 12 entries, one entry for each month. But if the month is February (ie, its value is 2) and if the year is a leap year (ie, it is evenly divisible by 4), then you will need to add 1 to the number of days (28). If the following logical expression produces a true result, then 1 should be added to the number of days:

```
MONTH @ 2 =  YEAR @ 4 MOD 0= AND
```

WORD	STACK	ACTION
AND	f1 f2 -- f3	Returns true if flags f1 and f2 are both true.
OR	f1 f2 -- f3	Returns true if either flag f1 or f2 (or both) is true.
NOT	f1 -- f2	Returns true if flag f1 is false, and false if it's true.

Conditional structures

Logical operators record information about circumstances or conditions in the form of true/false Boolean flags, which they leave on the stack. We can then use these flags to select among alternative choices of action. Let's write a word that will examine a flag and do different things depending on what it finds. If the flag is true, it will print "true"; if it is false, it will print "false." Here's how you set it up:

```
: TRUTH   IF ." TRUE  " ELSE ." FALSE " THEN  ;  OK
```

The word IF removes and examines the flag on top of the stack. If it is true, IF continues executing the words which follow until it reaches ELSE; if it is false, IF skips ahead to continue execution with the first word which follows ELSE. In either case, execution continues with the words following THEN, if any. Try out TRUTH with some comparisons:

```
10 3 > TRUTH TRUE  OK
10 3 < TRUTH FALSE  OK
```

It is often helpful to diagram these alternate pathways--this is particularly true as the choices grow more complicated. We'll use a simple method (based on the "D-charts" developed by Professor Edsger W. Dijkstra) to display what we've just done.

In this method, the name of the word we are diagramming, along with its stack diagram, appears at the top, over a horizontal line. The path that this word follows as it executes (called the "flow of control") starts at this line and always moves downward (with one exception, as we will later discover). When a condition leads to a decision, the alternate pathways are separately labeled.

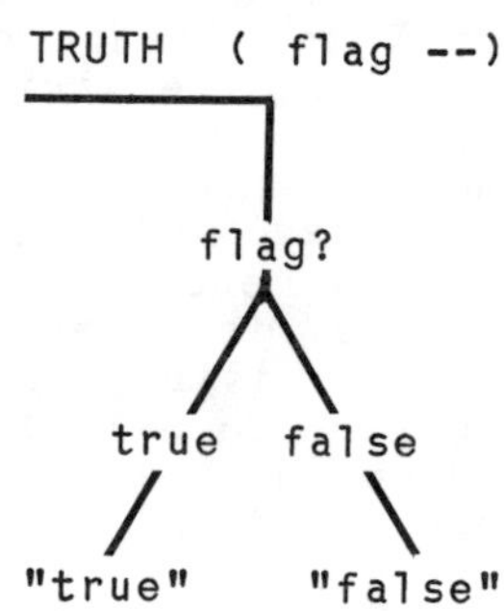

It doesn't matter which side is true. When a pathway ends, control is understood to leave the diagrammed word. The stack must be in its final form at this time.

In some cases, the ELSE alternative is simply to do nothing. In that case, take it out--it's optional. An example of a situation like this is a word that checks the stock of some item (say, boxes of detergent) in a supermarket. If the number of boxes goes below some number, called a "reorder point," then a message prompting the user to reorder is displayed. If there are enough items in stock, no action is taken. Let's make 12 the reorder point for all items. You could start by creating a constant equal to 12:

```
12 CONSTANT REORDER-POINT  OK
```

The word IN-STOCK compares the number of boxes in stock with the constant:

```
: IN-STOCK   ( #items --- )
  REORDER-POINT < IF ." TIME TO REORDER " THEN  ;

15 IN-STOCK  OK
10 IN-STOCK  TIME TO REORDER  OK
```

Now let's get back to the craps game and see what else these conditional structures can do:

Once you have rolled the dice and added the total, you need to examine the total and make some decisions. One thing you might do is print the message "Craps! You lose" if you roll a total of 2 (snake eyes) or 12 (boxcars) on the first throw.

```
: SNAKE-EYES   ( total --)
  2  = IF ." CRAPS! YOU LOSE " THEN ;  OK

: BOXCARS      ( total --)
  12 = IF ." CRAPS! YOU LOSE " THEN ;  OK
```

Test these words with a reasonable total (from 1 to 12, just as you would get with two dice) and see if they work:

```
2 SNAKE-EYES  CRAPS! YOU LOSE  OK
5 SNAKE-EYES  OK
12 BOXCARS    CRAPS! YOU LOSE  OK
```

Since you need to perform two tests on the same total, you should DUP the total first:

```
: CRAPS   ( die1 die2 --- )
  + DUP SNAKE-EYES BOXCARS ;
```

These words illustrate the importance of modularity: CRAPS is made from the two modules SNAKE-EYES and BOXCARS, each of which has simple, yet clearly defined actions. You could have redefined SNAKE-EYES to include the DUP, thereby making the definition of CRAPS shorter, but this would have limited the usefulness of SNAKE-EYES in other situations where a copy of the total was not necessary. Remember, _words should do as little as possible_.

Other truths

Conditional structures (such as IF--THEN and IF--ELSE--THEN) will react to any non-zero value as if it were a true (-1) flag:

```
25 TRUTH TRUE OK
-3 TRUTH TRUE OK
```

This is especially useful in programming situations where you want to do something if there is a non-zero quantity and otherwise want to do nothing.

Look again at the word INTO which you defined in chapter 3. It took an assortment of change, converted it into pennies, and redistributed them into the highest coin denominations. But in a real program situation, there might not be any change to redistribute. How would you tell FORTH to execute INTO only if it found change left over on the stack? You can write a new word, ?INTO, to check for this:

```
: ?INTO   ( change --- )
  DUP IF INTO ELSE DROP THEN ;
```

Note that you had to DUP the number on the stack before checking it; if you didn't, IF would have removed the number, and there wouldn't have been a copy left for INTO to work with. If the number representing the amount of change was 0, however, there would still be a copy of it left after ELSE was executed, so a DROP is necessary to leave the stack clean.

This situation comes up so often in FORTH that a special word, ?DUP ("question-dup"), has been written to factor out the inevitable DROP. It DUPs the top number on the stack only if it's true. Just for fun, one possible definition of ?DUP is:

```
: ?DUP   DUP IF DUP THEN  ;
```

Naming conventions

In FORTH, words which expect a flag on the stack are given a name which begins with a question-mark, such as ?INTO and ?DUP. Words which print results have names which include a [.], like .S and [."]. There are other naming conventions in FORTH, but these two are used the most often.

Here is an improved version of ?INTO using ?DUP:

```
: ?INTO   (change --- )
?DUP IF INTO THEN ;
```

Look again at CRAPS. On the first throw, you would roll the dice and check for a total of 2 or 12. But if the total is 2, there's <u>no need</u> to check to see if it's also 12. Since the categories are mutually exclusive, it makes no sense to check for both. This is even more important when you have more things to check for; for example, in some versions of craps, a sum of 3 on the first throw also loses.

What you need in a case like this is a system of "nested" conditional structures. (To make the system even more efficient, try to factor out the repetitive elements of the structure before you try nesting. In this case, we can isolate the losing message in a word called SORRY!:

```
: SORRY! ." CRAPS! YOU LOSE! " ;
```

Notice how SORRY! fits into the following structure:)

```
: CRAPS2  (die1 die2 --)
  + DUP 2 =
  IF SORRY!
  ELSE DUP 3 =
     IF SORRY!
     ELSE 12 =
        IF SORRY!
        THEN
     THEN
  THEN ;
```

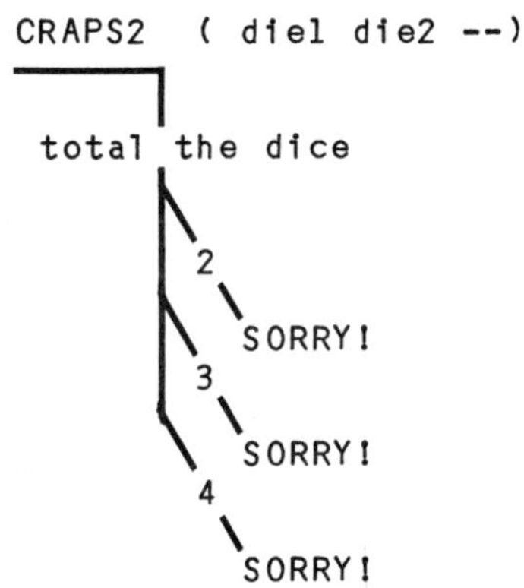

Note the indentations in the program. As in an outline, the conditional structures are contained within each other, like boxes within boxes. Such indentation can become very complicated. In a real game of craps, for example, you have to check for 2 or 12 or 3 (the losing combinations) and 7 and 11 (the winning combinations)-- <u>five</u> mutually exclusive possibilities. Notice in the following example how the rearrangement of words makes the program easier to read.

To complete the craps program for the first throw you will need a winning message:

```
: WIN!   ." YOU WIN!" ;  OK
```

You'll also need a variable to hold the total "point" in case the game continues:

```
VARIABLE POINT  OK
```

Here is the completed program:

```
: FIRST-THROW  ( die#1 die#2 --- )
  +  ( only the total counts )
  DUP  2 = IF SORRY! ELSE
  DUP 12 = IF SORRY! ELSE
  DUP  3 = IF SORRY! ELSE
  DUP  7 = IF   WIN! ELSE
  DUP 11 = IF   WIN! ELSE
  POINT !    ( otherwise)
  THEN THEN THEN THEN THEN ;  OK
```

Try out this "multiple-choice" control structure:

```
2 1 FIRST-THROW  CRAPS! YOU LOSE!  OK
6 1 FIRST-THROW  YOU WIN!  OK
3 2 FIRST-THROW  OK
POINT ? 5  OK
```

WORD	STACK	ACTION
IF	flag --	Used in a definition in the form IF--ELSE--THEN or simply IF--THEN. If flag is true,
ELSE		the words following IF are executed (but the words following ELSE are skipped).
THEN		If false, the words following ELSE are executed (if the ELSE part exists). exists).
?DUP	n -- 0 -- n n	Duplicates n if it is non-zero.

Exercises

1. Now that you have learned the comparison, logical, and flow of control operators, define MAX and MIN.

2. Given 0< and 0=, define 0> and 0<>.

3. Define the new logical operator, NAND, in terms of the current logical operators AND, OR, and NOT. NAND returns false if both of its operands are true--otherwise it returns true:

```
0  0 NAND . -1  OK
-1 0 NAND . -1  OK
0 -1 NAND . -1  OK
-1 -1 NAND . 0  OK
```

4. For advanced students: given NAND, define the other logical operators AND, OR, and NOT. Use these words to define the "exclusive-OR" (XOR) logical operator. Hint: the formula for XOR is given by:

```
([(not-B) and A] or [(not-A) and B])
```

   where A and B are Boolean flags.

5. Complete the definition of DAYS described in this chapter. To test DAYS, store month and year values into the variables MONTH and YEAR and check your results:

```
4 ( APRIL) MONTH !  1980 YEAR !  OK
DAYS .  30 OK
```

   Don't forget to test February on a leap year.

6. Here's a number-guessing game for you to program. The computer starts with a secret number from 1 to 100. You try to guess the number. With each guess, the computer responds "WARMER" if the new guess is closer than the old one, and "COLDER" if it is not. If you guess within 2 of the number, you're "HOT," and if you guess the number exactly, you're told how many guesses you took. The action looks something like this:

```
GAME  OK  ( Sets the secret number.)
10 GUESS COLDER  OK
80 GUESS WARMER  OK
75 GUESS HOT!  OK
73 GUESS
YOU WON IN 4 GUESSES!  OK
```

   Use RANDOM (from the last chapter) to set the secret number. What is a reasonable response to the first guess?

8 Loops

An extension of the idea of _taking_ an action _if_ a condition is true is to _repeat_ an action _until_ a condition is true. In flow-of-control terms, this is called an "indefinite loop." For example, in a dice game you continue to throw dice until you win or lose.

Indefinite loops

An interesting property of positive integers is revealed in the following program:

```
: WHATSIT  ( n --)
\ demonstrate a property.
  BEGIN
    DUP 2 MOD  ( is n odd?)
    IF  3 * 1+  ELSE  2/  THEN
    DUP .
    DUP 1 =
  UNTIL  DROP  ;
```

We will be showing you all definitions from this point on with appropriate comments and indentation. You may wish to enter all definitions into the file SAMPLE so you can experiment with them or correct any mistakes.

We can summarize the action of WHATSIT thus: " Pick a number. If the number is odd, multiply it by three and add one; if it's even, divide by two. Repeat with the result you obtain until the result equals one." The "interesting property" is that, although you are multiplying by three but dividing only by two, the result will eventually equal one. Here's a breakdown of the elements in WHATSIT:

WORD	STACK ACTION	
	n	The starting number.
BEGIN	n	Marks the beginning of an indefinite loop.
DUP	n n	Copies n.
2 MOD	n f	Flag is true if n is odd.
IF	n	Executes the following code IF flag is true; otherwise, skips to ELSE.
3 * 1+	n2	Multiplies n by 3 and adds 1. Skips to THEN.
ELSE	n	Executes the following code (IF flag was FALSE).
2/	n2	Divides n by 2.
THEN	n2	Marks the end of a conditional path. Both IF and ELSE continue here.
DUP .	n2	Copies n and then prints it.
DUP 1 =	n2 f	Creates a TRUE flag if n2 equals 1.
UNTIL	n2	Marks the end of an indefinite loop. If the flag is FALSE, execution will return to the most recently compiled BEGIN; otherwise, execution continues with the following code. In other words, execution repeats at BEGIN until the flag is TRUE.
DROP ;		Cleans the stack by DROPping the 1.

Enter WHATSIT from the keyboard (or LOAD it from a screen) and try it out:

```
40 WHATSIT 20 10 5 16 8 4 2 1  OK
25 WHATSIT 76 38 19 58 29 88 44 22 11 34
17 52 26 13 40 20 10 5 16 8 4 2 1  OK
```

In D-chart form, WHATSIT looks like this:

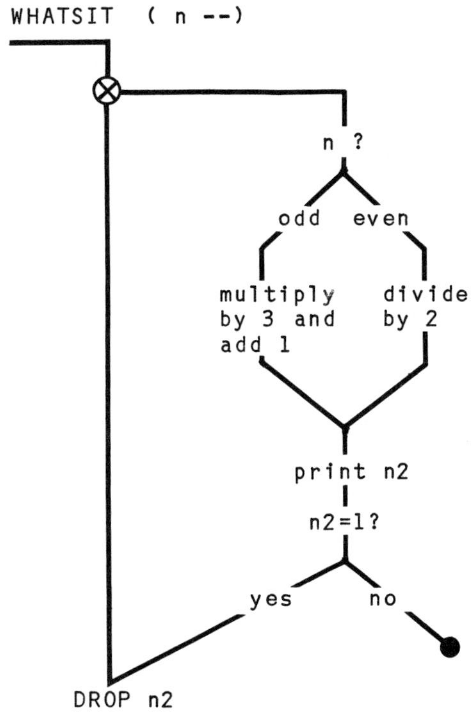

The BEGIN is marked with a large circled "X." The UNTIL is shown by a conditional test which exits the loop to the left if n2 equals 1; otherwise, the flow of control continues at the large black dot, which means "move upwards to the nearest BEGIN." The black dot and the circled X are borrowed from vector notation. They indicate that the flow of control is to travel at "right angles" to the other lines--in this case, into and out of the page.

In the BEGIN--UNTIL construct, the test that decides whether the program exits the loop is found at the bottom of the loop. This means that the code sequence within the loop will always be executed at least once:

```
1 WHATSIT 4 2 1 OK
```

An alternate form of the indefinite loop puts the loop test at the beginning. Look at this definition of CLEAR:

```
: CLEAR  ( ? --)
\ empties the stack.
  BEGIN  DEPTH
  WHILE  DROP
  REPEAT  ;
```

Here is CLEAR in more detail:

WORD	STACK	ACTION
	?	Anything could be on the stack here.
BEGIN	?	Marks the beginning of an indefinite loop.
DEPTH	? n	Leaves the number n of items on the stack, not including n itself.
WHILE	?	Executes the following if n is true, that is, if there are items on the stack (DEPTH > 0). If n is false, execution skips to the word following REPEAT. In other words, the program exits the loop when the stack is empty.
DROP	?	DROPs an item from the stack. The stack might now be empty.
REPEAT		Continues execution at the most recently compiled BEGIN.
;		Ends the definition. WHILE skips to here when it exits the loop.

And here is CLEAR in D-chart form:

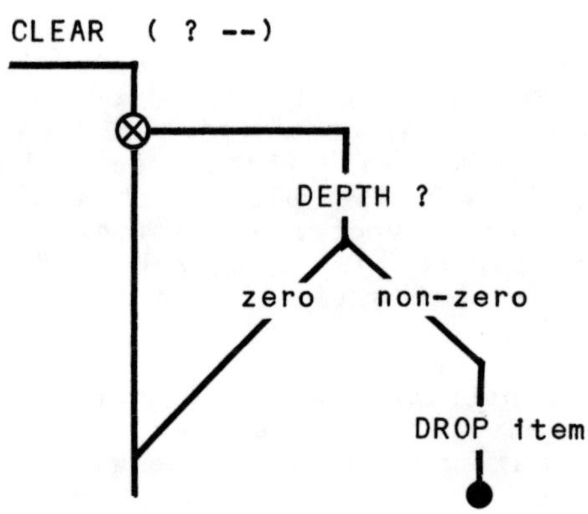

Ending the game

We now have all the programming elements we need to complete the dice game "craps." For your convenience, here is a copy of DICE and FIRST-THROW from the earlier chapters:

```
: DICE  ( -- die#1 die#2)
\ throws two die.
  6 RANDOM 1+  6 RANDOM 1+  ;
```

```
VARIABLE POINT  \ holds the "point" total.

: SORRY!  ( --)  ." CRAPS! YOU LOSE!"  ;
: WIN!    ( --)  ." YOU WIN!"  ;

: FIRST-THROW  ( die#1 die#2 --)
\ lose, win or continue.
  +  ( only the total counts)
  DUP  2 = IF SORRY! ELSE
  DUP 12 = IF SORRY! ELSE
  DUP  3 = IF   WIN! ELSE
  DUP  7 = IF   WIN! ELSE
  DUP 11 = IF   WIN! ELSE
  POINT !  ( otherwise)
  THEN THEN THEN THEN THEN ;
```

If the game continues beyond the first throw, you must keep throwing dice until the total of a throw is equal to your point (and you win) or else equals seven (and you lose). A BEGIN--UNTIL construct which plays the game might look like this:

```
BEGIN
  CR  DICE 2DUP . . +
  DUP 7 =   IF  SORRY! TRUE ( game over)  ELSE
  POINT @ = IF    WIN! TRUE ( game over)  ELSE
  FALSE ( otherwise keep playing)
  THEN THEN
UNTIL
```

BEGIN--UNTIL and BEGIN--WHILE--REPEAT, like IF--ELSE--THEN, are "compile-only" constructs. This means that, while you can compile them into a definition, you could never type them in directly from the keyboard. When we give an example like the one above, we do not expect you to try it out until it appears later within a definition.

TRUE and FALSE are constants. If your FORTH doesn't include them, their definitions are as follows:

```
0  CONSTANT FALSE  ( Boolean false)
-1 CONSTANT TRUE   ( Boolean true)
```

The TRUE and FALSE are necessary to inform UNTIL whether to continue playing or not.

The word EXIT lets us simplify situations like this in which we simply want to stop playing when the game is over. EXIT exits a definition immediately, no matter how deeply nested it is within BEGIN--UNTIL, BEGIN--WHILE--REPEAT, or IF-THEN-ELSE constructs. We can use EXIT to improve our game:

```
BEGIN
  CR  DICE 2DUP . .  +
  DUP 7 =    IF  SORRY! DROP EXIT ( game over)  THEN
  POINT @ = IF    WIN!       EXIT ( game over)  THEN
  FALSE
UNTIL
```

EXIT doesn't affect the stack, so we need DROP to remove the total of the dice if we lose. We need FALSE to tell UNTIL to keep playing. In fact, many FORTHs use the word AGAIN to replace FALSE UNTIL. AGAIN can be used to emphasize that the only valid exits from our dice loop are winning or losing:

```
BEGIN
  CR  DICE 2DUP . .  +
  DUP 7 =    IF  SORRY! DROP EXIT ( game over)  THEN
  POINT @ = IF    WIN!       EXIT ( game over)  THEN
AGAIN
```

And now, here is the completed craps program:

```
: CRAPS  ( --)
\ the game of craps.
  0 POINT !
  CR  DICE 2DUP . .  FIRST-THROW
  ( game won or lost on first throw?)
  POINT @  0= IF EXIT THEN
  BEGIN
    CR  DICE 2DUP . .  +
    DUP 7 =    IF  SORRY! DROP EXIT ( game over)  THEN
    POINT @ = IF    WIN!       EXIT ( game over)  THEN
  AGAIN  ;
```

The word EXIT cannot be used to improve FIRST-THROW because EXIT exits only the word it is in. Win, lose, or otherwise, FIRST-THROW must return to CRAPS when it is done. The variable POINT is used to communicate between FIRST-THROW and CRAPS. POINT will be set to the non-zero point total only if the game is to continue.

In D-chart form, CRAPS looks like this:

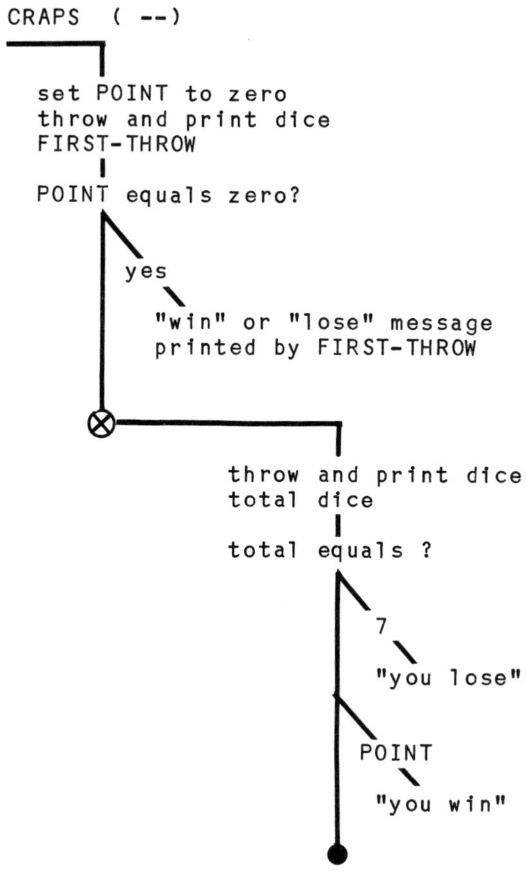

Finite loops

Finite loops are loops which are guaranteed to end after a certain number of repetitions. They are often used for counting or for repeating an action a given number of times. Look closely at the following example:

```
: SIX-SHOOTER ( --)
\ a simple DO--LOOP.
  6 0  DO  CR ." BANG!"  LOOP  ;

SIX-SHOOTER
BANG!
BANG!
BANG!
BANG!
BANG!
BANG! OK
```

DO--LOOPS must follow these rules:

- DO--LOOPs are compile-only constructs, and are always used within a definition.
- Every DO must have a LOOP, just as every IF must have a THEN.
- The "upper limit" of the loop (6) appears first in the structure.
- The "lower limit" or "index" (0) appears second. This number is incremented each time the loop is repeated.
- The actions to be executed appear between DO and LOOP.

The return stack

Before we continue our discussion of finite loops we need to look at the internal FORTH stack called the "return stack." FORTH uses this stack to keep track of program execution whenever one word calls another. For example, in the word CRAPS, before FORTH executes FIRST-THROW, it first pushes an address onto the return stack. This "return address" tells FORTH where in CRAPS to continue execution when it returns from FIRST-THROW. FORTH pops the return stack and returns to this address whenever it executes either a semicolon or an EXIT.

To avoid confusion, we will continue to call the normal FORTH stack the "parameter stack," or the "data stack," or simply the "stack." When we refer to the return stack, we will call it by its full name.

The return stack can come in quite handy as an extra stack. Three words are provided in FORTH to let you use this stack:

WORD	STACK	ACTION
>R	n --	"to-R" removes the top item from the parameter stack and pushes it onto the return stack.
R>	-- n	"R-from" removes the top item from the return stack and pushes it onto the parameter stack.
R@	-- n	"R-fetch" copies the top item of the return stack to the parameter stack.

If you use the return stack, you must use it carefully:

- >R, R>, and R@ should only be used within a definition.
- The return stack must be restored to its original state before leaving a definition with a semicolon or EXIT.

You can define a word which multiplies three coordinates by a scaling factor like this:

```
: 3DTIMES  ( x y z n -- nx ny nz)
  DUP >R * ROT
      R@ * ROT
      R> * ROT  ;
```

DO--LOOPS also use the return stack to keep track of the progress of the loop. Study this definition of SIGMA to see how the two stacks work together.

```
: SIGMA  ( n -- sum)
\ sum the integers from 0 to n-1.
  DUP 0= IF EXIT THEN ( exceptional case)
  0  ( running total)  SWAP 0  ( initial index)
  DO  I +  LOOP  ;

0 SIGMA . 0  OK
1 SIGMA . 0  OK   ( 0)
2 SIGMA . 1  OK   ( 0 + 1)
5 SIGMA . 10  OK  ( 0 + 1 + 2 + 3 + 4)
```

WORD	STACK	ACTION
	n	The upper limit plus 1.
DUP 0= IF EXIT THEN	n n 0	Does something reasonable if n is zero.
0	n 0	Initializes the running total.
SWAP 0	0 n 0	Establishes an initial count value (index) of 0 and an upper limit of n-1.
DO	0	Marks the beginning of the loop. The initial value and upper limit are moved to the return stack.
I	0 I	Copies the current index of the loop from the return stack to the parameter stack.
+	sum	Adds I to the running total.
LOOP	sum	Adds 1 to the current index (on the return stack). If the current index then equals the upper limit, the index and limit are removed from the return stack and execution continues with the next word; otherwise, execution returns to the most recently compiled DO.
;	sum	Ends the definition and returns to the address popped from the return stack, as usual.

DO--LOOPs can use D-charts too:

SIGMA (n -- sum)

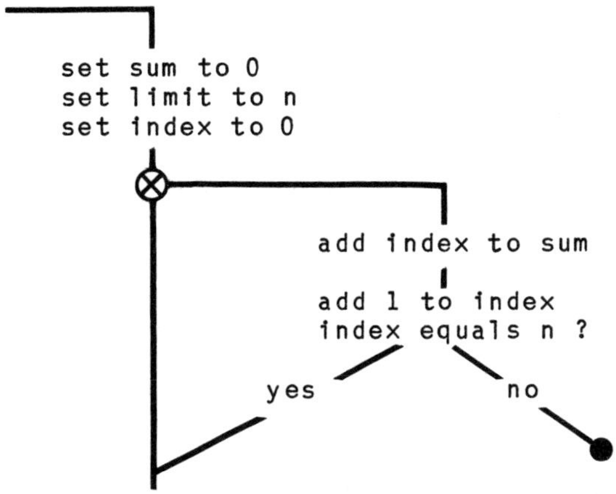

By using the return stack, DO--LOOPs don't clutter up the data stack with the index and limit of the loop.

The word +LOOP lets you increment the loop index by any integer. +LOOP is used like LOOP, except that it adds the number it finds on top of the stack to the loop index each time through the loop. For example, to count from 1 to 20 by 3, use the DO--+LOOP sequence in 20-BY-3:

```
: 20-BY-3  ( --)
  21 1  DO  I .  3 +LOOP  ;

20-BY-3 1 4 7 10 13 16 19  OK
```

+LOOP exits the loop when the index "crosses the boundary" between the limit minus 1 and the limit--that is, it stops the loop just after it increments the index from 19 to 21, which crosses the boundary between 20 (the limit 21 minus 1) and 21. In fact, the DO--LOOP is just a special case of the DO--+LOOP in which the increment is always one.

It's easiest to picture the action of LOOP and +LOOP if you think of the integer numbers arranged in a circle, with the largest possible integer connected to the smallest possible integer. When the loop prints the 19, +LOOP tries to move the index up 3 (to 22), but in the process it crosses the border between 20 (limit minus 1) and 21 (limit) and so does not return to the DO. Because LOOP checks only for boundary crossing, it can count and index memory addresses as easily as it counts integers.

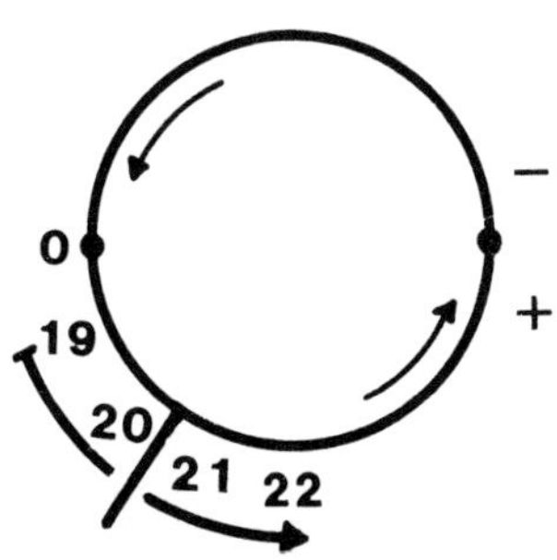

Such an image also helps explain why, when the loop parameters are set, the upper limit should always be a number greater than the index. If you set up loop parameters such as 3 and 3, for example, the loop would begin at 3 and continue around all possible integers until it stopped at 2, which is probably not what you had in mind.

Errors such as these can be tricky to spot. An incorrect definition of CLEAR using a DO--LOOP would be:

```
: CLEAR  ( ? --)
\ empties the stack.
  DEPTH 0 DO  DROP  LOOP  ;
```

This version of CLEAR correctly empties the stack as long as there are items to be DROPped. But if the stack is empty, the loop index and limit will both be 0, and far too many items will be dropped.

One way to fix this problem would be to insert an IF--THEN "clause" that would check the stack for 0 items before giving the go-ahead to run the loop:

```
: CLEAR  ( ? --)
\ empties the stack.
  DEPTH ?DUP IF 0 DO  DROP  LOOP THEN  ;
```

A shorter and neater way to handle the problem is to use the word ?DO ("question-do"), which will start a loop only if the upper limit is unequal to the initial index. With ?DO, CLEAR looks like this:

```
: CLEAR  ( ? --)
\ empties the stack.
  DEPTH 0 ?DO  DROP  LOOP ;
```

Nested loops

Loops, like IF--ELSE--THEN constructs, can be nested to any level. You could use a nested loop to take a list and compare each item in that list with each item in a second list. To do this, you will need both an inner and an outer loop index. The word I always gives you the innermost loop index, while the word J gives you the index of the next outermst loop. The word ODDS uses nested loops this way to examine probabilities in dice throwing.

```
: ODDS   ( sum -- n)
\ there are n ways to make sum by throwing 2 dice.
  0  ( the initial n) SWAP
  7 1
  DO  ( outer loop)
    7 1
    DO  ( inner loop)
       DUP I J + =  ( dice total=sum?)
       IF  SWAP 1+ SWAP  THEN
    LOOP
  LOOP
  DROP CR . ." OUT OF 36 WAYS "  ;

  4 ODDS
  3 OUT OF 36 WAYS  OK

  2 ODDS
  1 OUT OF 36 WAYS  OK
```

If you are nesting more than two loops, you will need to use variables or the data stack itself to hold a copy of the additional loop indices.

Leaving loops

DO--LOOP uses the return stack to hold the index and limit of a loop. This places two important restrictions on what can be done from inside a DO--LOOP:

- Any item pushed onto the return stack before entering the loop cannot be reached from inside the loop. The following sequence is meaningless:

```
>R  DO  R@ .  LOOP  R>
```

- Any item pushed onto the return stack after entering the loop prevents the loop index from being reached. The following sequence is also meaningless:

```
DO  0 >R  I .  R> DROP  LOOP
```

- The word EXIT cannot be used from inside a DO--LOOP. The return address cannot be reached.

You can, however, terminate execution of a DO--LOOP at any time with the word LEAVE. Before leaving a DO--LOOP, you must remove any items you have pushed onto the return stack from within the loop. LEAVE leaves the loop immediately, but does not exit the definition itself. You can use it to search an array for a match with a given key as follows:

```
CREATE KEEPERS  100 ALLOT  ( 50 cells)

: MATCH  ( key -- index true)( -- false)
\ find key in KEEPERS.
\ Returns index and true if key is found;
\ otherwise returns only false.
  FALSE ( assume no match) 50 0
  DO  DROP  DUP KEEPERS I + @ =  ( match?)
    IF  I SWAP TRUE LEAVE  THEN
    FALSE  2 ( two bytes per cell)
  +LOOP
  SWAP DROP  ( drops key)  ;
```

If the key is found, execution leaves the loop but remains in MATCH to drop the key. In the case of nested loops, LEAVE leaves only the loop which contains it.

WORD	STACK	ACTION

BEGIN
UNTIL
WHILE
REPEAT
	flag --	Used in a definition in the form BEGIN--UNTIL or BEGIN--WHILE--REPEAT. Marks the start of a word sequence for repetition. A BEGIN--UNTIL loop executes until flag is true; a BEGIN--WHILE--REPEAT loop executes until flag is false. When the loop finishes, execution continues with the word following the UNTIL or REPEAT.

EXIT	--	Exits a definition immediately.
AGAIN	--	Used with BEGIN in the form BEGIN--AGAIN to mark a word sequence for indefinite execution.
DO LOOP +LOOP	limit n -- incr --	Used in the form DO--LOOP or DO--+LOOP. Marks a word sequence for repetition until the loop index (initially n) crosses the boundary between the loop limit and the limit-1. LOOP increments the index by 1 with each repetition. +LOOP adds the increment on top of the stack to the index with each repetition. When the loop finishes, execution continues with the first word following LOOP or +LOOP.
I	-- i	Copies the loop index of the innermost loop to the stack.
J	-- j	Copies the loop index of the next outermost loop to the stack.
?DO	limit n --	Used in the form ?DO--LOOP or ?DO--+LOOP. ?DO, unlike DO, skips the loop if the initial index n equals the limit.
LEAVE	--	Leaves the innermost DO--LOOP or DO--+LOOP immediately, but does not leave the definition.

Exercises

1. The ACME Pack-Me company packs products into boxes. If a box of the proper size is not available, the next largest size will do. Boxes range in size from 0 to 9, and the following quantities are on hand (in the initialized array BOXES):

```
CREATE BOXES
3 , 2 , 0 , 4 , 0 , 1 , 4 , 2 , 2 , 3 ,
```

   In other words, there are currently 3 boxes of size 0, 2 of size 1, etc. Define a word BOX? which, when a box size is requested, returns the actual size to be used and decrements BOXES accordingly. It will look like this in action:

```
5 BOX? 5  OK  ( use size 5)
5 BOX? 6  OK  ( no more size 5 so use size 6)
```

   If there are no suitable boxes at all, BOX? will say so.

2. Write the word STARS which prints a given number of asterisks on a line:

```
6 STARS ****** OK
3 STARS *** OK
```

3. Define the utility word BOUNDS which, given a starting address and length in bytes, converts them to a form suitable for examining a range of addresses with a DO--LOOP. For example:

```
8050 ( address) 10 ( count) BOUNDS .S
8060 8050  OK
```

4. Write the word HISTOGRAM to display the elements of an array in histogram form. Histogram expects the starting address and number of cells in the array to be on the stack. For each cell, it prints a line of stars, the number of stars equal to the number in the cell. If you apply HISTOGRAM to the BOXES array from the first exercise, you would see:

```
BOXES 10 HISTOGRAM
***
**

****

*
****
**
**
*** OK
```

   Limit the number of stars to a reasonable value.

9 More on numbers

So far we have been working with 16-bit integer or "single-number" arithmetic. Most programming requires only integer arithmetic, even if you might think that the problem would require larger or more accurate numbers.

Numbers like 121.08 and 894 5/8 are called rational numbers; they aren't integers but can be expressed as the ratio of two integers. 121.08 is the same as 12108/100, and 894 5/8 is the same as ([8 * 894] + 5)/8 or 7157/8. In FORTH we can represent this second number in two ways:

```
894 5 8 / +
```

or

```
894 8 * 5 + 8 /
```

Either of these computations gives you 894, because the [/] function drops the fractional part of the quotient. Now try multiplying 894 5/8 by 2, using these two different computations (the exact answer is 1789.25).

```
894 8 * 5 + 8 / 2* . 1788  OK
894 8 * 5 + 2* 8 / . 1789  OK
```

What happened? In the first example, [/] dropped the fraction before the calculation was complete, and the answer came out too low. It's usually more accurate to divide after multiplying.

Another sort of calculation you may want to do is percentages. What is 37% of 182? To solve this on paper you would multiply 182 by 37 and divide by 100 to get 67.34. Let's write a FORTH word to do percentages:

```
: %   * 100 / ;  OK
182 37 % . 67  OK
```

So far, so good. Now try 37% of 1820 (it should be 673.4):

```
1820 37 % . 18  OK
```

What happened? The word [%] multiplied 37 by 1820, giving 67340. But this is larger than the largest positive single number, 32767, so a meaningless product was left on the stack.

Double numbers

What we need is a 32-bit number, or "double number," to hold the intermediate product until the calculation is complete. Double numbers range from -2,147,483,648 to +2,147,483,647. This range is large enough to hold any possible product of two 16-bit single numbers.

The FORTH-83 Standard double-number extension provides a rich set of double-number operations. We have already seen the stack manipulators 2DUP, 2DROP, 2SWAP, 2OVER, and 2ROT. We have also seen the memory operators 2!, 2@, 2CONSTANT, and 2VARIABLE. There are double-number equivalents to many of the other operators we have studied:

WORD	STACK	ACTION
D+	d1 d2 -- d3	d3 equals d1 plus d2.
D-	d1 d2 -- d3	d3 equals d1 minus d2.
DMAX	d1 d2 -- d3	d3 is the greater of d1 and d2.
DMIN	d1 d2 -- d3	d3 is the lesser of d1 and d2.
DABS	d1 -- d2	d2 is the absolute value of d1.
DNEGATE	d1 -- d2	Changes the sign of d1.
D2/	d1 -- d2	Divides d1 by 2.
D.	d --	Prints d.
D<	d1 d2 -- f	Returns true if d1 is less than d2.
D=	d1 d2 -- f	Returns true if d1 equals d2.
D0=	d1 -- f	Returns true if d1 is 0.
Many FORTHs also provide:		
D2*	d1 -- d2	Multiplies d1 by 2.

Given these operators, many others can be defined, for example:

```
: D>  ( dl d2 -- f)  2SWAP D<  ;
\ true if dl > d2.

: D<> ( dl d2 -- f)  D= NOT  ;
\ true if dl is unequal to d2.
```

When a double number is pushed on the stack, the most significant ("high-order") 16 bits are pushed on top of the least significant ("low-order") 16 bits. A single number can therefore be extended to a double number by pushing a -1 on top of it if it is negative or a zero if it is positive. The word S>D ("S-to-D") does exactly this:

```
: S>D  ( n -- d)
\ convert single to double number.
  DUP 0<  IF -1 ELSE 0 THEN  ;
```

In many FORTH's, ending a number with a decimal point automatically converts it to a double number.

```
1 S>D . . 0 1 OK
1 S>D D. 1 OK
1. D. 1  OK
700000. D. 700000  OK
```

When a double number is stored in memory, the high-order 16 bits are stored in the low-order memory cell:

```
2VARIABLE TWOSOME  OK
3 S>D TWOSOME 2! OK
TWOSOME 2@ D. 3  OK
TWOSOME @ . 0  OK
TWOSOME 2+ @ . 3  OK
```

The word [*/] ("star-divide") combines the multiplication and division we need for fractions or decimals but uses a double-number intermediate product to ensure accurate results. The divisor must be on top of the stack and the multiplier just underneath. Compare these two calculations:

```
15000 10 * 5 / . 3785  OK     ( wrong   )
15000 10 5  */ . 30000  OK    ( correct )
```

Let's rewrite [%] using [*/] :

```
: PERCENT   100 */ ;  OK

1820 37 PERCENT . 673  OK
```

We can also use [*/] to calculate the the area of a circle, given its radius. In FORTH we can't use 3.1416 for pi, but we can substitute 31416 / 10000. The formula for the area would then be:

```
: AREA ( radius -- area ) DUP *  31416 10000 */  ;
```

Surprisingly, it is possible to get even better precision by using 355/113 for pi instead of 31416/10000. Many mathematical constants can be expressed as the ratio of two single numbers.

Handy constants

constant	for decimal	substitute
pi	3.141592...	355/113
$\sqrt{2}$	1.414213...	19601/13860
$\sqrt{3}$	1.732050...	18817/10864
e	2.718281...	28667/10546
$\sqrt{10}$	3.162277...	22936/7253

Rounding

At times, we need to know how large the remainder of a division is. For example, this remainder might represent pennies left over from a compound interest calculation. Or we might need to examine the size of the remainder to determine whether we should adjust or "round" the quotient before we discard or "truncate" the remainder.

The word */MOD ("star-divide-mod"), like /MOD, leaves the remainder on the stack, just underneath the quotient; unlike [*/] , however, it uses a double-number intermediate product. We could then use the remainder to round a result to the nearest single number:

```
: ROUND%   100 */MOD SWAP 50 + 100 / + ;
```

Look at how this works with a real problem, say 15% of 3518:

STACK	ACTION
3518 15	Adds arguments to the stack.
100 */MOD	Multiplies 3518 by 15, giving an intermediate double number. Then it divides the product by 100, leaving a quotient (527) and a remainder (70) with the quotient on top. The remainder will be between 0 and 99.
SWAP	Swaps the quotient and the remainder so you can test the remainder for size.
50 +	Adds 50 to the remainder, leaving a sum between 50 and 149.
100 /	Divides modified remainder by 100, leaving a quotient of either 0 or 1 on the stack.
+	Adds new quotient to old quotient. If new quotient is 0 (that is, if the original remainder was less than 50) the old quotient remains unchanged; if the new quotient is 1 (that is, the original remainder was equal to or greater than 50) the old quotient is rounded up.

Check and see what your answer is:

```
3518 15 ROUND% . 528  OK
```

Sometimes you must round up. Say you are planning a school for 2430 students. You know that 7% of Americans are left-handed, and you want to plan for an adequate number of left-handed desks:

```
: ROUNDUP%   100 */MOD SWAP 99 + 100 / + ;  OK

2430 7 ROUND%   . 170  OK
2430 7 ROUNDUP% . 171  OK
```

Adding 99 to the remainder instead of 50 ensures that if there is any remainder at all, the program will round up the number.

Unsigned numbers

Signed integers are 16-bit numbers ranging from -32768 to 32767. The leftmost bit, called the "sign bit," indicates whether the number is positive or negative. This bit can be used instead as an ordinary number bit. The 16-bit unsigned number that results can represent the full range of 16-bit values from 0 to 65535.

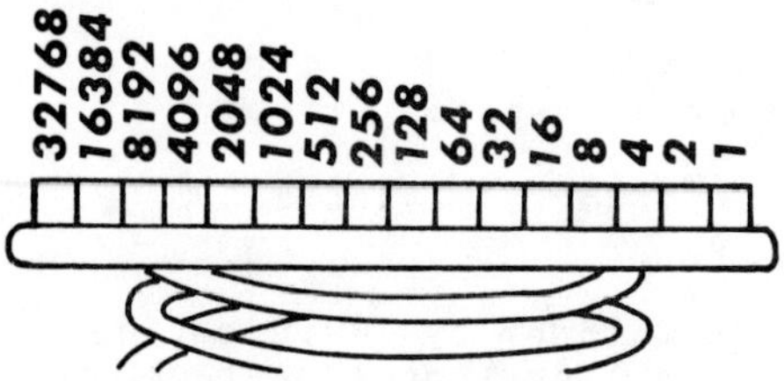

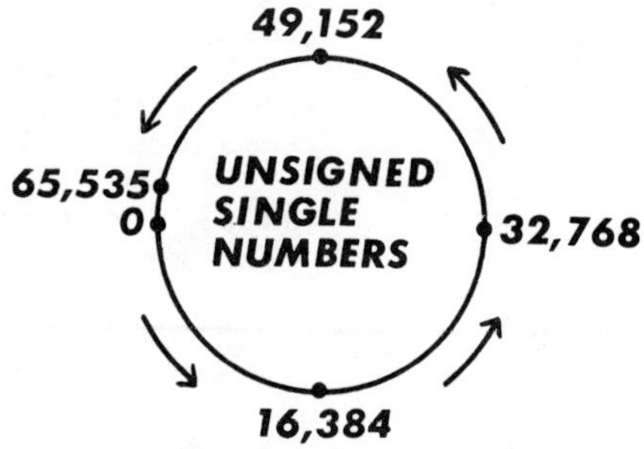

Whether or not a number is signed 16-bit or unsigned 16-bit is merely a question of how you look at it. To print a number as if it were unsigned, use U. ("U-dot") instead of [.] :

```
20000 20000 + .  -25536  OK
20000 20000 + U.  40000  OK

-1 U.  65535  OK
```

To create an unsigned number, just type it in:

```
40000 U.  40000  OK
```

Memory addresses are usually represented by unsigned numbers. That's why the memory "space" of most small computers is 65535 bytes or "64K" (one "K" is 1024 bytes--the tenth power of 2). Fortunately, the operators [+] and [-] work for both signed and unsigned numbers, so you can correctly add an offset to an address with [+] .

Many other single-number operators work correctly with unsigned numbers, such as = and 0=. Unfortunately, you can't compare two addresses with [<] .

```
30000 40000 < . 0  OK
```

That's because [<] "sees" 40000 as the signed integer -25536. Use U< ("U-less-than") instead:

```
30000 40000 U< . -1  OK
```

The unsigned operators required by the FORTH-83 Standard are:

WORD	STACK	ACTION
U.	u --	Prints an unsigned number.
U<	u1 u2 -- f	Returns true if u1 is less than u2.
DU<	ud1 ud2 -- f	Returns true if ud1 is less then ud2. This is the double-number equivalent to U<.
UM*	u1 u2 -- ud	Multiplies u1 by u2 to give the unsigned double-number product ud. All values are unsigned.
UM/MOD	ud u1 -- -- u2 u3	Divides the double number ud by u1 to give the quotient u3 and the remainder u2. All values are unsigned.

The mixed-number operators UM* ("U-M-times") and UM/MOD ("U-M-divide-mod") are the FORTH primitives for multiplication and division. They are usually faster than the equivalent signed operations when all values are known to be unsigned:

```
: FAST-TENTH  ( n1 -- n-remainder n-quotient)
\ quickly divides n1 by 10.
  0  ( forces n1 to be an unsigned double number)
  10 ( 10 can be considered to be unsigned, too)
  UM/MOD  ;

123 FAST-TENTH . . 12 3  OK
```

Changing bases

Decimal numbers are also called "base 10" numbers because they are based on the number 10. Computers usually translate decimal numbers to sequences of zeroes and ones ("bits"), which are called binary or "base 2" numbers. Sometimes you need to know exactly which pattern of bits a computer is using to represent a certain quantity. Rather than deal with long and often confusing binary numbers, you can group the bits four at a time into a single digit of the "hexadecimal" or "base 16" system ("hex" for short). Here are all 16 possible combinations of four bits:

binary		decimal		hex
0000	=	0	=	0
0001	=	1	=	1
0010	=	2	=	2
0011	=	3	=	3
0100	=	4	=	4
0101	=	5	=	5
0110	=	6	=	6
0111	=	7	=	7
1000	=	8	=	8
1001	=	9	=	9
1010	=	10	=	A
1011	=	11	=	B
1100	=	12	=	C
1101	=	13	=	D
1110	=	14	=	E
1111	=	15	=	F

Any 16-bit memory address can be represented by four hex digits. How many of these hex values do you recognize?

hex	decimal	
0000	0	The number 0.
00FF	255	The highest 8-bit (byte) value.
7FFF	32767	The largest positive signed 16-bit number.
8000	-32768	The largest negative signed 16-bit number.
FFFF	-1	The number -1.
FFFF	65536	The largest unsigned 16-bit number; also the highest 16-bit memory address.

FORTH uses a special variable called BASE to decide which numeric base to use for interpreting and displaying numbers. Normally, numbers are treated as decimal numbers. You can make sure this is true by using the word DECIMAL. Here is a probable definition for DECIMAL (assuming you are somehow working in decimal in the first place):

```
: DECIMAL   10 BASE !  ;
```

Some of these alternate base commands are probably also included in your dictionary:

```
: BINARY      2 BASE !  ;
: OCTAL       8 BASE !  ;
: HEX        16 BASE !  ;
```

Numeric conversion is easy in FORTH:

```
DECIMAL 35  CR DUP BINARY . HEX .
100011 23  OK
```

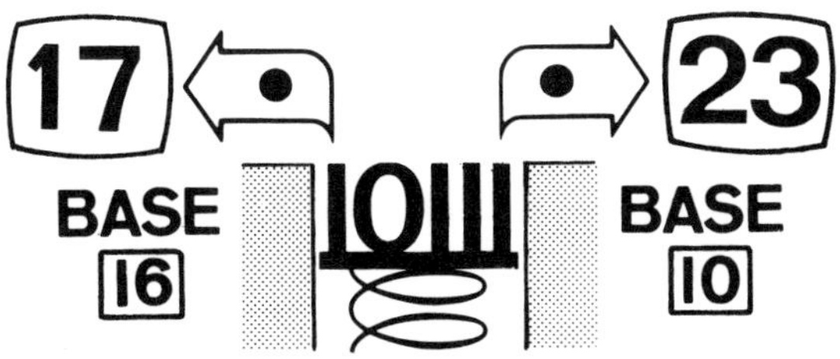

If you enter a number in hex, you should precede it with an extra 0 digit so that it doesn't accidentally look like something it shouldn't--better 0DEAD than DEAD.

Here are two useful words which use BASE. Both words fetch and restore BASE so that they can display numbers in a given numeric base without disturbing the current BASE. The first word prints the current numeric base in decimal:

```
: BASE?   ( -- )  BASE @  DUP DECIMAL .  BASE !  ;  OK

HEX       BASE?  16  OK
DECIMAL   BASE?  10  OK
```

The second word displays a range of bytes starting at a given memory address.

```
: DUMP   ( starting-address number-of-bytes -- )
  BASE @ >R  HEX           ( save BASE )
  CR  ." ADDR: " OVER U.   ( print starting address )
  CR  OVER + SWAP          ( print each byte )
    ?DO  I C@ U.  LOOP
  R> BASE !  ;             ( restore BASE )
```

If you were to DUMP the beginning of the POSTAGE-TABLE we created in an earlier chapter, you would see something like this:

```
POSTAGE-TABLE 8 DUMP
ADDR: 2B40
0 28 28 28 3C 50 64 78  OK
```

WORD	STACK	ACTION
*/MOD	n1 n2 n3 -- n4 n5	Multiplies n1 by n2, then divide by n3 leaving remainder n4 and quotient n5. Uses a double-number intermediate.
*/	n1 n2 n3 -- quot	Like */MOD, but leaves the quotient only.
BASE	-- addr	FORTH variable containing the value of the current numeric base for all input and output.
DECIMAL	--	Changes the current numeric base to decimal.

Exercises

1. Write the word GROWTH? which determines how many years it takes a number (use 1000) to double if it grows 15% per year. GROWTH? will look like this:

```
15 GROWTH? 5  OK
```

   1000 grows as 1150, 1322, 1520, 1748, and 2010.

2. The volume of a cone is given by the formula:

$$(PI * r^2 * h) / 3$$

   Define CONE (r=radius h=height -- area).

3. Define D>S which truncates a double number to a single number. The definition is surprisingly short.

4. Create the operator D~ which compares two double numbers for approximate equality. The amount by which the two numbers can differ and still be considered equal is stored in the variable FUDGE:

```
2 FUDGE !  OK
3 S>D 4 S>D  D~ . -1  OK
3 S>D 5 S>D  D~ . -1  OK
3 S>D 7 S>D  D~ . 0  OK
```

5. Write a smart .S which examines the current BASE and prints signed numbers if the base is decimal; otherwise it prints unsigned numbers:

```
DECIMAL CLEAR  OK
1 2 -3 .S
STACK: 1 2 -3  OK
HEX .S
1 2 FFFD  OK
```

10 Strings

Messages

We have already seen how . interprets the top stack item to be a signed integer, while U. interprets the same pattern to be an unsigned integer. The word EMIT interprets the top stack item as a printable character and prints it on the display:

```
HEX 41 . 41 OK
41 EMIT A OK
```

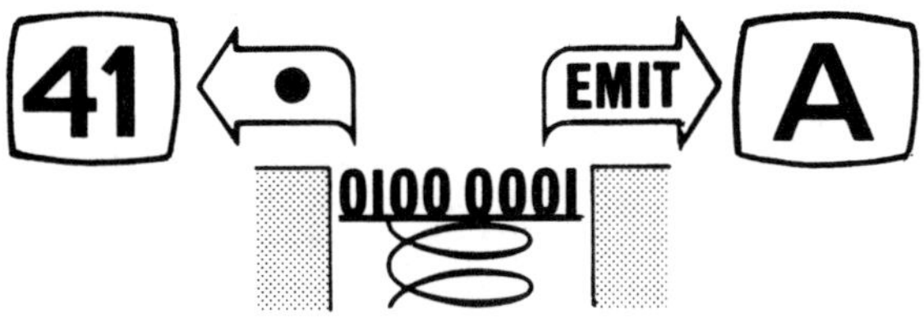

FORTH uses the 7-bit ASCII (American Standard Code for Information Interchange) patterns to represent printable characters. The high-order 9 bits are usually 0 but may have a system-dependent meaning, like "blink this character." A typical ASCII chart is given below:

ASCII Character set (7-bit codes)

LSD \ MSD	0	1	2	3	4	5	6	7
0	NULL		SP	0	@	P	`	p
1			!	1	A	Q	a	q
2			"	2	B	R	b	r
3			#	3	C	S	c	s
4			$	4	D	T	d	t
5			%	5	E	U	e	u
6			&	6	F	V	f	v
7	BELL		'	7	G	W	g	w
8	BACKSPACE	CANCEL	(	8	H	X	h	x
9	TAB		)	9	I	Y	i	y
A	LINEFEED		*	:	J	Z	j	z
B		ESCAPE	+	;	K	[	k	{
C	FORMFEED		,	<	L	\	l	|
D	RETURN		-	=	M	]	m	}
E			.	>	N	^	n	~
F			/	?	O	_	o	RUBOUT

To use this chart, locate the character you want to display. The column gives you the most significant hex digit (MSD), and the row gives you the least significant digit (LSD) of the ASCII code. For example, the code for lower case "z" is 7A (column 7, row A). The first printable character is the blank space (SP at hex 20).

The ASCII codes in the first two columns are for non-printing control characters. They are named after the corresponding printable character found by adding hex 40 to the control character. For example, 07 is called control-G. The control characters also have special names, some of which appear in the chart above. Hex 0A (control-J) is called LINEFEED, for example, because it is often used to reposition a cursor (or printer) to the left side of the current line. And on most terminals, the following definition causes an audible alarm (try it):

```
: BEEP  ( --)  \ make a beep.
  07 ( BELL = control-G) EMIT  ;
```

You can display all printable characters on your terminal with the word SEE-ALL:

```
DECIMAL
: SEE-ALL  ( --)  \ view all printable chars.
  128 32 DO I EMIT LOOP  ;
```

Many FORTHs support the command ASCII, which converts the character following it to an ASCII code and leaves it on the stack:

```
ASCII A  HEX . 41  OK
```

ASCII also works within a definition:

```
DECIMAL
: DASHED-LINE  ( --)  \ print a dashed line.
  14 0 DO ASCII - EMIT LOOP  ;

CR DASHED-LINE
-------------- OK
```

Note that the last definition is equivalent to this one::

```
: DASHED-LINE2  ( --)  \ print a dashed line.
  ." --------------"  ;
```

The `."` word is "compile-only", which means it can only be used within a definition. The equivalent word for use outside a definition is `.(` ("dot-paren"):

```
CR .( ECHO ME!)
ECHO ME!  OK
```

The word `.(` is useful for printing a message while LOADing a screen. Notice that it requires a matching `)` as the trailing delimiter.

Keyboard input

The input primitive of FORTH is KEY, which waits for a key to be pressed, then leaves the ASCII code for that key on the stack. Type in the following line, then press <RETURN>:

```
HEX KEY .
```

No OK appears. KEY is waiting for you to press a key, so press "A":

```
41  OK
```

FORTH accepts the key immediately and prints "OK."

If the ASCII code returned by KEY is larger than hex 7F, then some high-order bits have been set by your system. You can screen out or "mask off" these unwanted bits with 7F AND. The expression KEY 7F AND is guaranteed to leave a 7-bit ASCII code on the stack. We will talk more about masks and bit manipulation in a later chapter.

Try this simple word ECHO:

```
HEX
: ECHO  ( --)  \ echo each key until <RETURN>.
  BEGIN KEY 7F AND DUP EMIT 0D ( <RETURN>) =
  UNTIL  ;
```

Control-M (hex 0D) is the <RETURN> key. Type ECHO, then type "ABC" and press <RETURN>:

```
ECHO ABC
 OK
```

Many FORTHs also provide a word which checks to see whether a key has been pressed without waiting for one. The word is called KEY? , ?KEY , ?TERMINAL , or something similar, and leaves a flag which is true if a key has been pressed. You can use this word to allow yourself to interrupt a long loop by pressing a key:

```
DECIMAL
: ENDLESS  ( --)
\ print numbers until interrupted.
  10000 0 DO  I .  KEY? IF LEAVE THEN
          LOOP     KEY DROP  ;

ENDLESS 0 1 2 3 4 5 ( key pressed here)  OK
```

The KEY DROP sequence is used to clear the unwanted key.

FORTH also provides the word EXPECT which reads an entire line from the keyboard. EXPECT reads each key in turn and moves it to a memory buffer of your choice until either a <RETURN> is pressed or the buffer is full. The number of characters read is stored in the system variable SPAN. The <RETURN> itself is neither counted nor moved. EXPECT provides simple editing to allow the user to correct mistakes before hitting <RETURN>. This usually includes recognizing and handling the BACKSPACE (control-H) and CANCEL (control-X) keys. Let's write a simple routine to use EXPECT. We will need a buffer to hold the characters and a word to set up the arguments for EXPECT:

```
CREATE BUF  DECIMAL 80 ALLOT  ( 80-byte buffer)

: READLINE  ( --)
\ read a line into BUF.
  CR  BUF 80 ( addr size) EXPECT ;
```

Execute READLINE, then type "A SIMPLE LINE," followed by a <RETURN>:

```
READLINE
A SIMPLE LINE  OK
```

How many characters were read?

```
SPAN ? 13  OK
```

A routine very much like READLINE is used by the FORTH to read the next line of text to be interpreted. The characters are stored in the array whose address is given by TIB, and the count is stored in the system variable #TIB.

String representation

When READLINE reads a line from the keyboard to the buffer, a single 7-bit ASCII code is stored in each consecutive byte of the buffer, with the high-order bit cleared to 0.

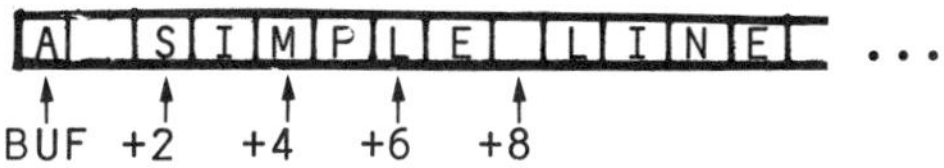

The expression BUF SPAN @ leaves the address of the first byte of the buffer BUF and the number of bytes actually read into BUF on the stack. These two arguments, starting address and length, exactly represent a consecutive sequence (or "string") of ASCII characters in memory. We will find it convenient to refer to this pair of arguments simply as a string. In stack notation, for example, we will say (string --) instead of (addr length --).

You can display a string with the command TYPE. TYPE the string in BUF out on your display:

```
BUF SPAN @ TYPE A SIMPLE LINE  OK
```

You could also have examined the string with DUMP, since DUMP expects the same arguments as TYPE, that is, starting address and length. In fact, strings are often used to represent arrays of bytes as well as sequences of ASCII characters.

Packed strings

Each string you read with READLINE replaces the previous string that was stored in BUF and SPAN. If you want to save a string, you must move the characters from BUF to another memory location. You must also save the character count, also called the string "length." The preferred format for saving strings is to store the length in the first byte of an array, followed by the characters in the string. Storing "A SIMPLE LINE" this way would look like this:

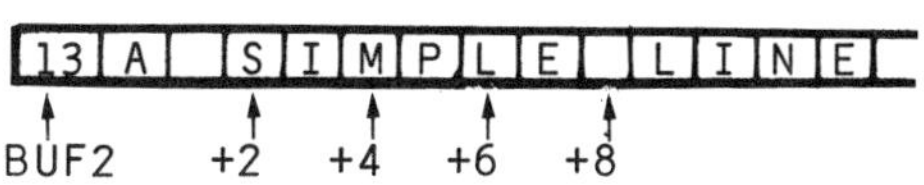

A string in this form is called a "packed string." Since only one byte is used to hold the length, the maximum length of a packed string is 255 characters. Zero-length strings are allowed and are called "null" strings.

The word CMOVE is the primitive for moving sequences of bytes from one memory location to another. CMOVE needs the "from" address, the "to" address, and the number of bytes to move. Let's create a second buffer and move the string in BUF and SPAN to it.

```
CREATE BUF2  80 ALLOT  ( same size as BUF)

BUF BUF2 1+ SPAN @ CMOVE OK  ( move the chars)
SPAN @ BUF2 C! OK            ( save the length)
```

This is even easier if you first define the word CPACK:

```
: CPACK  ( from-addr to-addr #bytes --)
\ move and pack a string with CMOVE.
  SWAP 2DUP C!  1+ SWAP CMOVE  ;
```

Here is the improved string move:

```
BUF BUF2 SPAN @ CPACK  OK
```

Now you can refer to a string simply by pushing the address of the packed string on the stack. An address used to refer to information this way is called a "pointer." We can say that the address left by BUF2 "points" to a packed string. The word COUNT converts a string pointer to a more useful string argument pair (starting address and length):

```
BUF2 COUNT TYPE A SIMPLE LINE  OK
```

COUNT is often defined this way:

```
: COUNT  ( ^string -- start-addr length)
\ convert a pointer to a packed string
\ to a string argument pair.
  DUP 1+ SWAP C@  ;
```

You can convert a string argument pair back into a string pointer with the expression DROP 1- , but only if you're sure that the string is packed.

Filled strings

CMOVE can be used to move any information from one memory location to another, one byte at a time. The byte at the lowest memory address (the "leftmost" byte) is moved first. If the "from" and "to" memory areas overlap, CMOVE may end up moving bytes which have already been moved.

You can exploit this effect to fill an arbitrary memory area with a repeating pattern of your choice. If you want to build a string of 10 stars in BUF, first put a star in the leftmost byte:

```
    ASCII * BUF C!  OK
```

Now CMOVE for 9 more bytes:

```
    BUF BUF 1+ 9 CMOVE  OK
```

Check your results:

```
    BUF 10 TYPE **********  OK
```

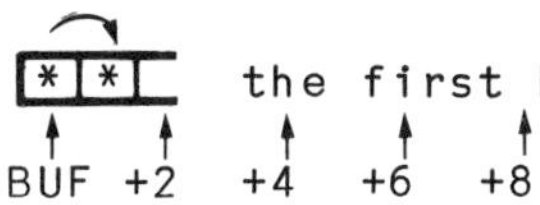

the first byte is moved.

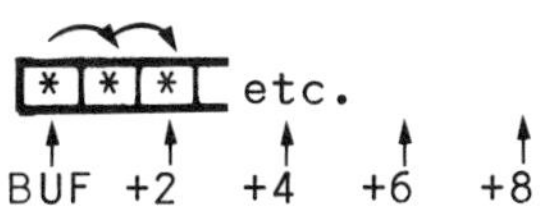

etc.

Here are some useful words based on CMOVE:

```
    : FILL  ( addr #bytes pattern --)
    \ fill memory with #bytes of pattern.
    \ Only the low-order byte of pattern is used.
      OVER 0= IF  DROP 2DROP EXIT  THEN
      SWAP >R  OVER C!  DUP 1+ R> 1- CMOVE  ;


    : ERASE  ( addr #bytes --)
    \ fill memory from addr with #bytes of zeroes.
      0 FILL  ;
```

To move a string safely when the "to" address is higher than the "from" address, use CMOVE> ("C-move-up"). CMOVE> is identical to CMOVE, except that the "rightmost" byte is moved first.

String manipulation

When a string is represented as a string argument pair, you can duplicate it with 2DUP and drop it with 2DROP. Bear in mind, however, that the string itself is not affected by the stack manipulation. 2DUP does not produce a duplicate copy of the string, nor does 2DROP destroy it. To make a true copy of a string, you must CMOVE or

CPACK it to another memory location.

Splitting a string into smaller parts is also easy when the string argument pair is on the stack. You can drop characters from the left side of a string by adding a constant to its starting address while decreasing its length by the same amount. Since "A SIMPLE LINE" is still in BUF2, let's drop the first two characters and print what remains:

```
BUF2 COUNT  SWAP 2+ SWAP 2- TYPE SIMPLE LINE  OK
```

The original string has not changed:

```
BUF2 COUNT TYPE A SIMPLE LINE  OK
```

Shortening a string this way is a common operation, and you might find the word /STRING handy:

```
: /STRING  ( string1 n -- string2)
\ drop the first n chars from a string.
  ROT OVER + -ROT -  ;
```

/STRING works like this:

```
BUF2 COUNT  9 /STRING TYPE LINE  OK
```

Dropping characters from the right of the string is even easier--just decrease the length:

```
BUF2 COUNT  5 - TYPE A SIMPLE  OK
```

These simple string operations can be combined to select any part of a string:

```
BUF2 COUNT 2 /STRING 5 - TYPE SIMPLE OK
```

Once a part of a string, called a "substring," is selected, it can be copied with CMOVE or CPACK to a separate memory area for further processing.

Here is a definition for the word -TRAILING, which "removes" trailing blanks from a string by shortening its length:

```
: -TRAILING  ( string1 -- string2)
\ effectively remove trailing blanks
\ by shortening a string.  The string
\ itself is not affected.
  DUP 0
  ?DO       ( examine each char, if any)
    2DUP + 1-  ( addr of the last char)
    C@ BL <>   ( is this char a blank?)
    IF LEAVE THEN ( no, so you're done)
    1-         ( shorten by one char)
  LOOP  ;
```

BL is a constant whose value is the ASCII code for a blank. If your FORTH doesn't have it, it can be easily added:

```
DECIMAL 32 CONSTANT BL  ( an ASCII blank)
```

String conversion

Single digits from 0 to 9 can be directly obtained from their ASCII codes (hex 30 to 39) by subtracting an ASCII 0. The following short program shows you how to prompt a user to select one of four items:

```
DECIMAL
: SELECT-IT  ( -- n)
\ pick an item from 0 to 3.
  BEGIN
    CR ." PLEASE SELECT AN ITEM:"
    KEY 127 AND DUP EMIT  ( echo)
    ASCII 0 -             ( convert)
    DUP 0< OVER 3 > OR    ( test range)
  WHILE
    ."  OOPS!" DROP
  REPEAT
  ."  THANK YOU"  ;
```

Converting a string of ASCII digits, such as you might obtain with EXPECT, to a number is somewhat more difficult. FORTH provides the primitive CONVERT, which converts a string of ASCII digits to a double number. Digits are converted from left to right and in the current numeric base. Note that "A" is a valid digit in the hexadecimal base but not in the decimal base. The string to be converted must end with a blank. The length of the string is ignored, and conversion stops when the first non-digit character is encountered. By calling CONVERT repeatedly and examining each character that it stops at, you can build sophisticated string-to-number conversion routines.

Let's construct a conversion routine that accepts a string of ASCII digits and converts it to a double number. The string can optionally be preceded by a minus sign but can contain no other punctuation. Since you cannot assume that the string ends with a blank, you must arrange to add one. You must first copy the string to a temporary area and then add the blank. FORTH provides such a temporary area for string storage, called PAD. The following sequence copies a string to PAD and prepares it for CONVERT:

```
PAD SWAP CPACK       ( copies the string to PAD)
BL PAD COUNT + C!    ( adds a blank)
```

CONVERT requires a double-number accumulator on the stack, initialized to zero, and the starting address to be converted, minus one. CONVERT returns the double-number result and the address of the first non-digit character. Here is the word VAL, which sets up and calls CONVERT:

```
: VAL  ( string -- dn true)
\ converts a string to a double number.
\ True if conversion ends successfully on a blank.
  PAD SWAP CPACK      ( copies the string to PAD)
  BL PAD COUNT + C!   ( adds a blank)
  0 0                 ( double-number accumulator)
  PAD                 ( starting address minus 1)
  CONVERT  ( dn1 addr1 -- dn2 addr2)
  DUP C@ ASCII - =    ( leading minus sign?)
  IF   CONVERT        ( continue conversion)
       >R DNEGATE R>  ( negative case)
  THEN  C@ BL = ;     ( successful conversion?)
```

Use READLINE to read a string, then use VAL to convert it to a number:

String ->	flag	(dn)	comment
DECIMAL			Set base to decimal.
"123"	-1	123	Successful conversion.
"12A"	0		"A" is not a digit.
HEX			Set base to hexadecimal.
"12A"	-1	12A	"A" is now a digit.
"54,321"	0		"," is not allowed.
"-12ABC"	-1	-12ABC	Successful conversion.

Number conversion

You have already seen how to type numbers with the "dot" operators (., D., and U.). At times, you may want to add punctuation or otherwise control the way that a number prints. FORTH provides a flexible set of primitives to convert a double number to a string. Once you have a string, you can reformat it before printing it. And since single signed and unsigned numbers can be easily converted to double numbers, a number can be printed in any way you like.

The FORTH double-number conversion primitives are:

```
<#   "less-sharp"
 #   "sharp"
 #S  "sharp-S"
 #>  "sharp-greater"
```

HOLD and SIGN

The symbols <# and #> are used as brackets to signal the beginning and end of conversion. As the conversion progresses, a string is constructed by the operators #, #S, HOLD, and SIGN. When the conversion is complete, #> pushes the address and length of this string on the stack. A possible definition for a word to print an unsigned double number would be:

```
: DU.  ( u --)
\ print an unsigned double number.
  <# #S #>  TYPE SPACE  ;
```

The sequence <# #S #> converts the number to a string, which is then printed by TYPE. The word #S converts all of the digits to characters in the string. No leading zeroes are printed unless the number is 0, in which case a single "0" is printed. The command SPACE prints an extra space. FORTH provides both SPACE and SPACES, with these possible definitions:

```
: SPACE  ( --)  \ print a space.
  BL EMIT  ;

: SPACES  ( n --)  \ print n spaces.
  0 MAX  0 ?DO SPACE LOOP  ;
```

The word SIGN adds a minus sign (an ASCII -) to the string if the number on top of the stack is negative. The definition of D., which prints a signed double number, would be something like this:

```
: D.  ( d --)
\ print a double number.
  DUP  -ROT DABS  ( save the sign)
  <# #S ROT SIGN #>
  TYPE SPACE  ;
```

The conversion words expect an unsigned double number to be on the stack. To convert signed numbers, you need a sequence like the one above to save and restore the sign for SIGN. Conversion proceeds from right to left, starting with the least significant digit, so SIGN is often the last word in the conversion sequence.

You can add punctuation as you convert with the word HOLD. HOLD takes an ASCII character and adds it to the string. Suppose you are programming a business application. Money in cents is represented by a signed double number. To print an amount of money, you will want, from right to left, two digits for the cents amount, a decimal point, the dollar amount, and a leading dollar sign. Here is a word that will do this for you:

```
: .MONEY  ( d --)
\ print money.
  DUP -ROT DABS
  <# # # ASCII . HOLD #S ASCII $ HOLD ROT SIGN #>
  TYPE SPACE  ;
```

Each # forces the conversion of one digit, even if the number is zero:

```
0 0       .MONEY $0.00  OK
12345.    .MONEY $123.45  OK
-999 S>D  .MONEY -$9.99  OK
```

To print numbers in even columns, you can use the length of the string returned by #> to determine how many extra spaces should be printed on the left. The word D.R, defined below, right-justifies a number in a column of a given width. If the width is too small for the number, the width is ignored and the full number is printed:

```
: D.R  ( d width --)
\ print d right-justified
\ in a field of the given width.
  >R  DUP -ROT DABS
     <# #S ROT SIGN #>
  R> OVER - SPACES TYPE  ;
```

Print a column of numbers with D.R:

```
CR 0. 5 D.R  CR 123. 5 D.R  CR -2. 5 D.R
    0
  123
   -2  OK
```

Most of the number printing words can be based on D.R:

```
: D. ( d --)  0 D.R SPACE  ;
: U. ( u --)  0   D.  ;
: .  ( n --)  S>D D.  ;
```

The conversion words build a string in a temporary area (usually just under PAD). Since there is only one temporary area, a converted string should be printed or moved to a string buffer before the next conversion is begun. This is why the definitions we have given TYPE the string immediately after conversion. With care, however, you can work directly with the string before printing it. Suppose you define (D.) to convert a signed double number to a string. You can base both D. and D.R on (D.) as follows:

```
: (D.)  ( d -- string)
  DUP -ROT DABS  <# #S ROT SIGN #>  ;

: D.    ( d --)  (D.)  TYPE SPACE  ;
: D.R   ( d width --)
  >R (D.) R>  OVER - SPACES TYPE  ;
```

String extensions

Many FORTHs include additional string commands for creating, storing, and comparing strings. Some FORTHs use a string stack, while others compile strings directly into definitions. We will present some typical string extensions here which are based, in large part, on the commands you have learned so far.

The defining word STRING creates a string buffer of a given maximum size:

```
DECIMAL 20 STRING ALPHA  OK
```

This line creates the string buffer ALPHA, which can hold a string of up to 20 characters. Actually, 22 bytes are allocated to ALPHA: the first byte holds the buffer size (20), and the second byte holds the current string size (initially 0, since the buffer is empty).

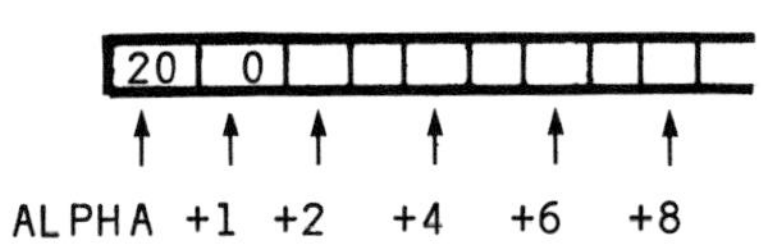

Unlike a simple byte array, however, ALPHA leaves a string on the stack by doing a COUNT on the second byte of its array (the length byte). In this case, the starting address of the string will point to the third byte of the array.

array.

A specific string, called a "string literal," can be created by enclosing the string with double-quote marks. Like ." , the string must be separated from the leading double quote by a blank. Here is a string literal for the word "FORTUITOUS":

```
" FORTUITOUS" TYPE FORTUITOUS  OK
```

The TYPE is used to show that the string is on the stack in correct form: starting address and length. Double quotes can be imbedded in the string by doubling them:

```
" ""QUOTED""" TYPE "QUOTED"  OK
```

String literals can be used within definitions, in which case the string is stored directly in the definition. String literals used outside of definitions are stored in a temporary area, usually PAD. Therefore, only one string literal can be created outside a definition at a time--if you want to save it, you must move it to a safe area, such as a string buffer created by STRING. The word S! ("S-store") will let you do this. S! expects to find two strings on the stack: the string literal, and the string left by a string buffer. By backtracking from the address of the string buffer, S! finds the buffer size and truncates the string if necessary:

```
: S!  ( string1 string2 --)
\ stores string1 into string2.
\ String2 must be left by a string buffer.
  DROP 1- DUP 1- C@  ( backtrack to buffer size)
  ROT MIN CPACK  ;
```

```
" A SHORT STRING" ALPHA S!  OK
ALPHA TYPE A SHORT STRING  OK
" A STRING LONGER THAN 20 CHARACTERS" ALPHA S!  OK
ALPHA TYPE A STRING LONGER THAN  OK
```

A variation of S! can be used to concatenate one string to another.

```
: S+  ( string1 string2 --)
\ concatenates string1 to string2.
\ String2 must be left by a string buffer.
  ROT >R  OVER 1- 2DUP 1- C@
  SWAP - R> MIN
  SWAP OVER >R +!  ( add lengths)
  + R> CMOVE  ;
```

```
" EAST SIDE" ALPHA S!  OK
ALPHA TYPE EAST SIDE  OK
" , WEST SIDE" ALPHA S+  OK
ALPHA TYPE EAST SIDE, WEST SIDE  OK
```

Two strings can be compared with the word COMPARE. COMPARE returns -1 if the first string is "less than" the second, 0 if they are equal, and 1 if the first string is "greater than" the second. "Less than" means that the string would appear first in a dictionary, that is, in lexicographical order. Let's walk through the definition of COMPARE to see how it works:

WORDS	**ACTION**
: COMPARE	(string1 string2 -- -1 or 0 or 1)
ROT 2DUP >R >R	Saves the lengths.
MIN	Limits # of chars to compare (#comp).
TRUE	Assumes equality, soon to be dropped.
SWAP	(^text1 ^text flag #comp)
0 ?DO	Compares by character, #comp times.
DROP	Drops flag.
OVER C@	
OVER C@ =	Compares these characters.
IF	If equal, continues comparing.
1 1 D+	Increments the text pointers.
TRUE	Assumes equality again.
ELSE	If unequal,
FALSE LEAVE	comparison is complete.
THEN	
LOOP	(^text1 ^text2 flag)
IF 2DROP	If equal, length determines order.
R> R> 2DUP =	Compares lengths.
IF 2DROP 0	If equal, strings are equal too.
ELSE >	Determines which is greater.
2* 1+	Transforms TRUE to -1 and FALSE to 1.
THEN	
ELSE	If unequal, lengths are unnecessary.
R> R> 2DROP	Drops lengths.
C@ SWAP C@ >	Compares the unequal characters.
2* 1+	Transforms TRUE to -1 and FALSE to 1.
THEN ;	Comparison is complete.

Try comparing two strings with COMPARE. Since only one string literal is allowed outside of a definition, first move the other string to ALPHA:

```
" IMPORT" ALPHA S!  OK
" EXPORT" ALPHA COMPARE . -1  OK
" IMPORT" ALPHA COMPARE . 0  OK
" IMPORTANCE" ALPHA COMPARE . 1  OK
```

WORD	STACK	ACTION
KEY	-- char	Reads an ASCII key.
EMIT	char --	Displays an ASCII key.
KEY?	-- f	True if key pressed.
EXPECT	addr n --	Reads up to n chars or <RETURN> into the buffer at addr.
SPAN	-- addr	Variable which contains the number of chars from the last EXPECT.
PAD	-- addr	Points to a temporary buffer.
TIB	-- addr	Points to the FORTH terminal input buffer.
#TIB	-- addr	Variable which contains the number of chars in TIB.
CMOVE	addr1 addr2 n --	Moves n bytes from addr1 to addr2, leftmost byte first.
CMOVE>	addr1 addr2 n --	Moves n bytes from addr1 to addr2, rightmost byte first.
FILL	addr n pattern --	Fills n bytes with low-order byte of pattern, starting at addr.
COUNT	^string -- string	Unpacks string. Length byte byte is at ^string. Chars begin at ^string+1.
TYPE	string --	Displays a string.
CONVERT	d1 addr1 -- d2 addr2	Converts string at addr1+1, accumulating number into d1. Stops at first non-digit char (at addr2).
SPACE	--	Prints a space.
SPACES	n --	Prints n spaces.
D.R	d n --	Prints double number d left-justified in a field n wide.
-TRAILING	string1 -- string2	Removes trailing blanks from string1.

WORD	STACK	ACTION
<#	d -- d	Initializes for numeric conversion.
#	d1 -- d2	Converts one digit of d1.
#S	d -- 0 0	Converts all remaining digits.
HOLD	char --	Adds char to conversion string.
SIGN	n --	Adds "-" to conversion string if n is negative.
#>	d -- string	Ends conversion, leaving string.

String extensions:

WORD	STACK	ACTION
ASCII	--	Used in the form: ASCII c. The ASCII code of the following char c is left on the stack.
CPACK	addr1 addr2 n --	Moves and packs a string from addr1 to addr2 of length n.
VAL	string -- d f	Converts a string to a double number. True if conversion succeeds.
/STRING	string1 n -- string2	Drops n leftmost chars of string1.
STRING	n -- -- string	Creates a string buffer n bytes long. In use, leaves the string currently in the buffer on the stack.
" ccc"	-- string	Creates the string literal ccc, delimited by double-quote marks.
S!	string1 string2 --	Stores string1 in string2. String2 must be left by a STRING buffer.
S+	string1 string2 --	Appends string1 to string2. String2 must be left by a STRING buffer.
COMPARE	string1 string2 -- -1|0|1	Compares string1 to string2. Returns -1 if string1 less than string2 in lexicographical order, 0 if equal, and 1 if greater than string2.

Exercises

1. Write the word <CMOVE> which (unlike CMOVE or CMOVE>) safely moves an array of bytes either upward or downward in memory, even if the source and destination overlap.

2. Write WAIT-KEY, which waits in a loop for a key to be struck, incrementing the variable KEY-DELAY each time through the loop. KEY-DELAY could be used to initialize a random number generator.

3. If your FORTH supports lower-case entry and display, define the word UPPER to convert a string to upper case. UPPER should only affect characters in the range of "a" to "z." If a string has a length 0, it should be properly ignored.

4. Using CONVERT, write the word NUMBER, which converts a string to a double number. If a decimal point appears anywhere in the string, its location is saved in the variable DPL (decimal point location). If no decimal point appears, DPL is set to -1.

```
" 12345"  NUMBER D. DPL ? 12345 -1  OK
" 12345." NUMBER D. DPL ? 12345 0  OK
" 12.345" NUMBER D. DPL ? 12345 3  OK
```

5. Define the word LEX, which splits a string into two at a given delimiter. The delimiter is removed and either string can be null (length 0). LEX is useful for breaking strings into meaningful substrings:

```
" VOLUME:NAME" ASCII : LEX  OK
TYPE NAME  OK     ( right string)
TYPE VOLUME  OK   ( left string)
```

6. Using the conversion words <# # #S SIGN HOLD and #>, Redefine D. to insert a comma between each three digits, starting from the right. Your new definition of D. will act like this:

```
1234567. D. 1,234,567  OK
```

For advanced students:

7. Define the pattern-matching primitive IN. IN looks for one string within another. If the string is found, IN returns the position of the first match and a true flag; otherwise IN returns only a false flag. Assuming you have string extensions like the ones described in this chapter, IN would be used in this way:

```
" PATTERN" ALPHA S!  OK
" PAT" ALPHA IN . . -1 0  OK ( found in pos# 0)
" ATT" ALPHA IN . . -1 1  OK ( found in pos# 1)
" XYZ" ALPHA IN . 0  OK      ( not found)
```

11 Defining words

We have seen how the defining words :, CONSTANT, VARIABLE, and CREATE can be used to add new words to your dictionary.

> The most powerful programming tool you have in FORTH is the ability to define new defining words.

Sounds confusing? Don't panic. Most of the work is already done for you by the words CREATE and DOES>.

Compile-time action

You have seen how CREATE can be used to build variables, arrays, and tables. In the way of review, let's use CREATE to build a two-dimensional array or "matrix." A matrix can be "unraveled" into a normal one-dimensional array by allocating the first row in memory, followed by the second, and so forth. Suppose you want to build a "3 by 5" (3 rows of 5 columns) array of bytes. To find the third cell of the second row, you would skip 5 bytes (the first row) from the beginning of the matrix, and then skip two more (the first two columns of this row). This can be expressed by the formula:

```
^item = ^matrix + ([row# * #cols] + col#)
```

where

```
row#    = row number
col#    = column number
#rows   = number of rows    (= bytes/column)
#cols   = number of columns (= bytes/row)
^matrix = starting address of matrix
^item   = address of item at row# and col#
```

A matrix of bytes is completely described by its two dimensions: bytes/row and bytes/col. The dimensions must be remembered somehow when the matrix is created. The defining word MATRIX does all of this for you:

```
: MATRIX  ( #rows #cols --)( -- ^matrix)
\ define a #rows by #cols byte matrix.
  CREATE
    2DUP , ,  ( remember the dimensions)
    * ALLOT   ( #rows * #cols elements)  ;
```

You haven't actually created any matrices yet. But you have specified what will happen when you do. The first comment (#row #cols --) reminds you that when MATRIX is executed, it expects to find the two dimensions of the matrix on the stack. CREATE creates the matrix and each , compiles a dimension into the dictionary for later use. The ALLOT then allocates one byte for each element of the matrix. So the "compile-time" action of MATRIX is to create the matrix by compiling the dimensions and allocating space for the elements

The second comment (-- ^matrix) tells you that when any matrix is executed ("runs"), it will leave the address of the first cell of data compiled into the dictionary--in this case, #cols. This is exactly the run-time action of CREATE. In fact, this is the default run-time action for any new word created by a defining word. This makes sense when you realize that there's no point in compiling data into the dictionary if you can't find them afterwards.

Use MATRIX to make a 3 by 5 matrix:

```
3 5 MATRIX BOXES  OK
```

What's on the stack now? Nothing yet! The defining word MATRIX has been executed. Its compile-time action is to create the matrix BOXES.

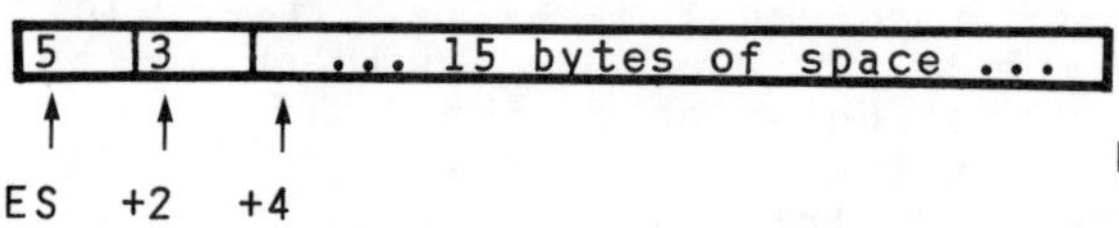

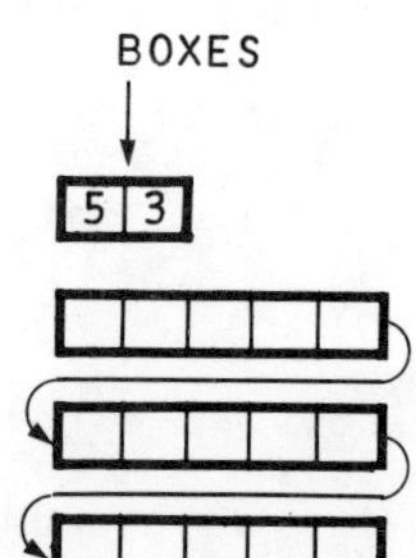

The dimensions 3 and 5 are compiled into the dictionary and 15 bytes of storage are allocated for the elements of the matrix.
Only the word MATRIX has run, and not the matrix BOXES.
Be sure you understand this before reading further.

The run-time action of BOXES is to leave the address of the first cell of the matrix on the stack, which contains the dimension "number of columns":

```
BOXES ? 5  OK
```

If you're not sure where this number came from, try rereading the section on arrays.

You could say that BOXES is a member of the "class" matrix, created by the defining word MATRIX.

> Separating the compile-time action of the defining word from the run-time action of the defined word is the key to understanding defining words.

With the address returned by BOXES you can define a word which will find the address of any element within BOXES, given its row and column number. Bear in mind that when you count items in FORTH, you usually start from zero:

```
: ELEMENT  ( row# col# ^matrix -- ^element)
\ finds the addr of the element at row# and col#.
  DUP >R @  ( retrieve #cols = bytes/row)
  ROT * +   ( apply formula for offset)
  R> 4 +    ( addr of first element)
  +  ;
```

See if it works:

```
DECIMAL
100  0 2 BOXES ELEMENT C!  ( 1st row, 3rd col)
150  1 1 BOXES ELEMENT C!  ( 2nd row, 2nd col)

0 2 BOXES ELEMENT C@ . 100  OK
1 1 BOXES ELEMENT C@ . 150  OK
```

By using CREATE, we can create data structures of any complexity. This is because we can use the full power of FORTH (including other defining words) to compile the data in whatever form we wish.

Run-time action

The default run-time action of any word created by CREATE is to leave the address of the internal data storage area (called the "body") of the word on the stack. The size, format, and initial contents of this area are determined by the words which follow CREATE in the defining word. For example, here is a definition for the defining word VARIABLE:

```
: VARIABLE  ( --)( -- addr)
\ creates a variable.
  CREATE  0 ,  ;
```

Using this definition, any variable of the class VARIABLE will have a one-cell body initialized to zero. When the variable is executed, it will leave the address of this body on the stack.

Once the address of the body of a word is known, the data stored within the body are available for further processing. The word DOES> lets you specify the run-time action to be done on these data by the defined word itself. In other words, DOES> lets you extend the default run-time action of any defined word. Here is a definition of the word VALUE which is identical to the FORTH word CONSTANT:

```
: VALUE  ( n --)( -- n)
\ creates a constant.
  CREATE ,
  DOES>  @  ;
```

Be sure you understand what is happening and when. The compile-time action of VALUE is to CREATE a word with a one-cell body initialized to the value n, which is on the stack when the word is defined:

```
CLEAR  OK
5 VALUE FIVE  OK
```

At this point, the defining word VALUE has run, but the defined word FIVE has not. What's on the stack right now?

```
STACK: EMPTY  OK
```

Normally, you would expect that FIVE, or any word created by CREATE, would leave the address of its body on the stack. In this case, when FIVE runs, you would expect to find the address of the body of FIVE, which contains the number 5, on the stack. However, the DOES> within VALUE extends this default action with a @, so that the value (5) in the body is returned rather than its address.

```
FIVE . 5  OK
```

You can use DOES> to make the run-time action of MATRIX "smarter." Simply incorporate the action of ELEMENT within the definition of MATRIX:

```
: SMART-MATRIX
\ defines a #rows by #cols byte matrix.
\ Finds the addr of the element at row# and col#.
  CREATE ( #rows #cols --)
    2DUP , ,  ( remember the dimensions)
    * ALLOT   ( #rows * #cols elements)  ;
  DOES>  ( row# col# -- ^element)
    DUP >R @  ( retrieve #cols = bytes/row)
    ROT * +   ( apply formula for offset)
    R> 4 +    ( addr of first element)
    +  ;
```

The stack diagrams for compile-time and run-time action follow the CREATE and DOES> words, respectively. You will find this smarter matrix easier and more natural to use:

```
3 5 SMART-MATRIX COLLECTOR OK

100  0 2 COLLECTOR C!  OK
150  1 1 COLLECTOR C!  OK

0 2 COLLECTOR C@ 100  OK
1 1 COLLECTOR C@ 150  OK
```

You could have redefined MATRIX instead of renaming it to SMART-MATRIX. The old version of MATRIX, however, is functionally different from the new version. "Functionally different" means that the two words differ either in the arguments they expect or the results they produce. It is potentially confusing for two functionally different versions of a word to have the same name.

> Whenever you change the function of a word, give the new version a new name.

You can use DOES> to add error or limit checking to a class of words. This version of SMART-MATRIX uses MAX and MIN to keep the row and column numbers within the bounds of the matrix:

```
: SMARTER-MATRIX
\ defines a #rows by #cols byte matrix.
\ Finds the addr of the element at row# and col#.
\ Limits the row# and col# to lie within the matrix.
  CREATE ( #rows #cols --)
    2DUP , ,  ( remember the dimensions)
    * ALLOT   ( #rows * #cols elements)  ;
  DOES>  ( row# col# -- ^element)
    DUP  >R    @ 1- MIN 0 MAX  ( limit col#)
    SWAP R@ 2+ @ 1- MIN 0 MAX  ( limit row#)
    SWAP R@ @  ( retrieve #cols = bytes/row)
    ROT * +    ( apply formula for offset)
    R> 4 +     ( addr of first element)
    +  ;
```

FORTH allows you to add error checking to words but does not require that you do so. Contrast this with other programming languages, which use extensive error checking even when it is not needed.

All objects which can be represented in computer memory fall into one of two classes: data and operations to be done on data. Most programming languages allow you to design and create data structures, sometimes called "records" or "types." Similarly, they allow you to group data operations into "subroutines," "modules," "functions," or "programs." The FORTH construct CREATE--DOES> lets you define a class of "objects" by specifying both the data organization and the data operation for objects of that class. You can think of an object as either a smart data structure or as a program with built-in data storage. The structure and behavior of an object is conveniently presented by CREATE--DOES> in the definition of the defining word for that object.

> FORTH's ability to define a class of objects with CREATE--DOES> is its single most powerful feature.

Compilation addresses

Sometimes you need to define a word before you know what its definition should be! You might be designing a word which calls several other words, not all of which have been written yet. You could define dummy words or "stubs" to indicate the undefined words and then replace them with final definitions later. Or suppose you want to write a simple version of a word, to be replaced with a more sophisticated word when necessary. There is a way to apparently defer and otherwise manipulate the run-time action of word in FORTH.

Normally, when you compile a definition, the address of each word wich appears in the definition is compiled into the dictionary. This "compilation address" tells the FORTH interpreter where to begin executing a word. You can find the compilation address of a word with the command ' ("tick"), followed by the name of the word. For example, executing ' DUP leaves the compilation address of DUP on the stack. You can then execute the word at this address with the word EXECUTE. So the sequence ' DUP EXECUTE does the same thing as DUP.

```
CLEAR 1 2 3  ' DUP EXECUTE  .S
STACK: 1 2 3 3  OK
```

You can save the compilation address in a variable for

future use, as in the following example:

```
: THING1  ." FIRST ACTION" ;  OK
: THING2  ." SECOND ACTION" ;  OK

VARIABLE ACTION  OK

' THING1 ACTION !  OK
ACTION @ EXECUTE FIRST ACTION  OK

' THING2 ACTION !  OK
ACTION @ EXECUTE SECOND ACTION  OK
```

Notice that you are using a clearly defined operation (@ EXECUTE) on the data (the compilation address) in the variable ACTION. This suggests that you can make a defining word to describe words like ACTION. Consider this definition of DEFER:

```
: DEFER
\ create a deferred definition.
  CREATE  ( --)
    2 ALLOT
  DOES>   ( ?)
    @ EXECUTE  ;
```

The compile-time action of DEFER is to create a deferred word, whose action will be specified later:

```
DEFER SURPRISE  OK
```

SURPRISE, like all objects of the class DEFER, has internal storage for one compilation address. The run-time action of SURPRISE is to retrieve and execute this compilation address.

Parameter addresses

Unfortunately, we can't initialize or change the action of SURPRISE because we no longer know the location of its body, where the compilation address is normally stored. This is because the address of the body (also called the "parameter address") is used by the sequence DOES> @ EXECUTE in DEFER and is no longer available to us.

The solution to this problem is to use the command >BODY ("to-body") to change the compilation address of a word into its parameter address. Once you know the parameter address of a word, you can directly access the data stored in the word. Now you can set the action of SURPRISE like this:

```
' THING1  ' SURPRISE >BODY !  OK
SURPRISE FIRST ACTION  OK

' THING2  ' SURPRISE >BODY !  OK
SURPRISE SECOND ACTION  OK
```

>BODY can be used to access the body of any word. You can use it to examine and change the value of the word FIVE defined earlier:

```
' FIVE >BODY ? 5  OK
4 ' FIVE >BODY !  OK
FIVE . 4  OK
```

It is even possible to change the value of a constant this way, although a FORTH-83 Standard program is not allowed to do so.

> If you are interested in a value which often changes, use a VARIABLE. If it seldom changes, use a VALUE, and if it never changes, use a CONSTANT.

You can use ['] within a definition, but this can lead to one of the most confusing constructs in FORTH:

```
: CONFUSION
\ planned obfuscation.
  ' THING1 DROP ;

CONFUSION THING2 FIRST ACTION  OK
```

What happened? The compilation addresses of ['], THING1, and DROP were compiled into the definition of CONFUSION in the usual manner. When CONFUSION was executed, ['] ran, leaving the compilation address of the following word, which was then THING2, on the stack. Then THING1 ran, printing "FIRST ACTION." Finally, DROP dropped the compilation address of THING2, which was never used.

The word ['] ("bracket-tick") is a variation of ['] for use within a definition. Its usage is best illustrated with an example. Let's use it to improve DEFER to print a warning if an uninitialized definition is executed:

```
: WARNING  ( --)
  ." UNINITIALIZED"  ;

: DEFER
\ improved deferred definition.
\ Warns of uninitialized definitions.
  CREATE  ( --)
    ['] WARNING ,
  DOES>   ( ?)
    @ EXECUTE  ;
```

The new DEFER works like this:

```
DEFER FORGOTTEN  OK
FORGOTTEN UNINITIALIZED  OK

' THING1 ' FORGOTTEN >BODY !  OK
FORGOTTEN FIRST ACTION  OK
```

The ['] in DEFER compiles the compilation address of the following word WARNING as a "literal" number. This means that when DEFER FORGOTTEN is executed, ['] will push the compilation address of WARNING on the stack. This is used by [,] to initialize the body of FORGOTTEN to the WARNING.

You can improve the readability of a sequence like ' NAME >BODY ! with the word IS:

```
: IS  ( value --)
\ sets the body of the following word to value.
  ' >BODY ! ;
```

Read this definition carefully. This is exactly the case which we described above in the CONFUSION example. The word IS can be used to set the value of any body:

```
' THING2 IS FORGOTTEN  OK
FORGOTTEN SECOND ACTION  OK

10 IS FIVE
FIVE . 10  OK
```

This definition of IS cannot be used within a definition. We will present a better definition of IS in a later chapter.

Positional case

An array or table of compilation addresses lets you assign an action to an array index. The idea of relating a number to an action is sometimes called "vectored execution" and appears in programming languages as "positional case statements," "GODO" constructs, or something similar. In the following example, television channel numbers are each given an action. The action could be to set an electronic tuner, but in this case, we will simply have it print out a channel identification. MAX and MIN are used to ensure that something reasonable is done even for meaningless channel numbers:

```
: KNXT  ." KNXT" ;
: KNBC  ." KNBC" ;
: KTLA  ." KTLA" ;
: KABC  ." KABC" ;
: KHJ   ." KHJ " ;
: KTTV  ." KTTV" ;
: KCOP  ." KCOP" ;
: N/A   ." NO STATION" ;

CREATE CHANNELS
  ' N/A  ,  ' N/A  ,  ' KNXT ,  ' N/A  ,
  ' KNBC ,  ' KTLA ,  ' N/A  ,  ' KABC ,
  ' N/A  ,  ' KHJ  ,  ' N/A  ,  ' KTTV ,
  ' N/A  ,  ' KCOP ,  ' N/A  ,


: CHANNEL ( channel# --)
\ identify a TV channel using CHANNELS.
  0 MAX 14 ( decimal) MIN 2* ( bytes/cell)
  ['] CHANNELS >BODY +
  @ EXECUTE  ;

-1 CHANNEL NO STATION  OK
 0 CHANNEL NO STATION  OK
 1 CHANNEL NO STATION  OK
 2 CHANNEL KNXT  OK
 3 CHANNEL NO STATION  OK
 4 CHANNEL KNBC  OK
99 CHANNEL NO STATION  OK
```

WORD	STACK	ACTION
DOES>	-- -- parm-addr	Used in the form: : <class> ... CREATE ... DOES> xxx ; then <class> ccc extends the run-time action of the new word ccc to include the code sequence xxx.
' ccc	-- comp-addr	Leaves the compilation address of the word ccc on the stack.
['] ccc	-- comp-addr	Like ['], but for use within a definition only. When the definition runs, leaves the compilation address of the word ccc which followed it in the definition.
EXECUTE	comp-addr --	Executes a word given its compilation address.
>BODY	comp-addr -- parm-addr	Converts a compilation address into a parameter (body) address.

Exercises

1. Write the defining word STRING described in the chapter on strings. The compile-time action of STRING (n --) is to create a string-buffer for a string up to n bytes long. The run-time action of a string buffer (-- string) is to leave the string it contains on the stack.

2. Design the defining word COUNTER. When it is executed, an object of the class COUNTER increments an internal counter. You will need a word RESET to initialize the counter and a word EXAMINE to print its value:

   ```
   COUNTER KILROY  OK
   RESET KILROY OK
   KILROY KILROY KILROY  OK
   EXAMINE KILROY 3  OK
   ```

   You can put counters like this in words to see how many times they've been executed.

3. Write 2VALUE--the double-number equivalent of VALUE. Be sure 2VALUE stores the high-order cell of the number in the low-order cell of the body.

4. Assume the variable COLOR-REGISTER represents a hardware register for setting the color of text on a graphics screen. Write a defining word which creates colors. The run-time action of a color is to store its value into COLOR-REGISTER:

   ```
   4 COLOR YELLOW  5 COLOR VIOLET  OK

   YELLOW COLOR-REGISTER? 4  OK
   VIOLET COLOR-REGISTER? 5  OK
   ```

5. Write the defining word POINT which stores the two-dimensional coordinates of a point. When a point runs, these coordinates are multiplied by the value SCALE before being pushed on the stack:

   ```
   10 12 POINT OBJECT1  8 13 POINT OBJECT2  OK

   1 IS SCALE  OK
   OBJECT1 . . 12 10  OK

   2 IS SCALE  OK
   OBJECT1 . . 24 20  OK
   OBJECT2 . . 26 16  OK
   ```

12 Compiler words

Every word in the FORTH dictionary has a name and a body. The name is stored at the beginning of the word in an area called the "name field." The body of the word is also called its "parameter field." In addition, each word has a "link field" and a "code field." Together, these four fields completely describe the word.

Name and link fields

The name and link fields are built by CREATE when a new word is first defined. All of the defining words use CREATE to create and name new words. CREATE reads the name which follows it and moves it to the end of the dictionary, preceded by a length byte. Enough bytes are reserved to hold the name and its length byte, which are together called the "name field."

In addition, two more bytes are reserved for an address pointer or "link" to a previous word. By following these "link fields" from one word to the next, FORTH can find any word in the dictionary. The first word in a chain of links has a link-field value of 0. In some FORTHs, the link field precedes the name field, and in others, it follows. Some FORTHs point the link field to the name field of the previous word. In fact, links can be completely rearranged to increase the speed of searching for a word in the dictionary.

Let's suppose that HERE is at hexadecimal address 1000 when you create the new word EXAMPLE:

```
CREATE EXAMPLE
```

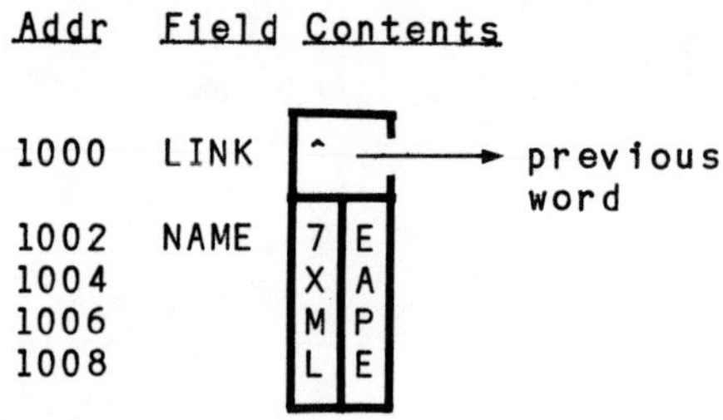

We will use the up-arrow symbol ("^") to mean "a pointer to something." Notice that the structure of the name field strongly resembles that of a packed string. Name fields, however, differ from packed strings in two important ways:

1. Names are limited to 31 characters. The length occupies at most 5 bits of the length byte, and the remaining 3 bits have system-dependent values.

2. The length stored is the original or "natural" length of the name. The number of characters actually stored is set by the system variable WIDTH.

WIDTH normally has the value 31, meaning that all characters in a name are saved. You can save dictionary space by setting WIDTH to a lower value:

```
3 WIDTH !  OK
CREATE EXACTING  OK
```

The name field of EXACTING looks like this:

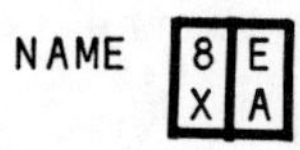

FORTH can still distinguish between EXAMPLE and EXACTING because they have different natural lengths.

WORDS knows how to display natural lengths:

```
WORDS
EXA_____
EXAMPLE
...
```

The 5 underscores are FORTH's way of saying that it knows EXACTING has 8 letters but only remembers the first three. New words are not always as fortunate as EXACTING:

```
CREATE EXAMINE
EXAMINE ISN'T UNIQUE  OK
```

FORTH can't tell the difference between EXAMPLE and

EXAMINE because both the natural length and all the characters stored in the EXAMINE name field match those of EXAMPLE:

```
NAME  | 7 | E |
      | X | A |
```

The smaller you set WIDTH, the more space you save, but the more likely you will be to have name conflicts. A compromise is to set WIDTH to 31 while you are writing your application program:

```
31 WIDTH !  OK
```

When the program is finished, reduce WIDTH as much as you can without causing name conflicts.

Code and parameter fields

The code field of a word generally follows the name field and tells FORTH what the word is to do. The link, name, and code fields (but not the parameter field) are created by CREATE when a word is defined. The code field always contains the address of machine code to be run when the word is executed. Here is a complete diagram of the fields in EXAMPLE (created above):

```
Addr  Field  Contents

1000  LINK   | ^     | ----> previous
                             word
1002  NAME   | 7 | E |
1004         | X | A |
1006         | M | P |
1008         | L | E |

100A  CODE   | ^     | ----> (VAR) machine-code
```

The code field points to a machine-code routine called (VAR), DOVAR ("do-variable"), or something similar. When EXAMPLE is executed, FORTH will transfer control to (VAR), which is the default run-time code for any word defined by CREATE. When (VAR) finishes executing, it returns to FORTH at a special address called NEXT.

The normal action of (VAR) is to push the address of the parameter field (the body) of a word onto the stack. However, since we neglected to allocate any memory storage for the parameter field, the address returned will be meaningless. We could recreate EXAMPLE and add a one-cell parameter field with 2 ALLOT. Or we could recreate it as a VARIABLE, which builds exactly the same fields:

```
FORGET EXAMPLE  OK
VARIABLE EXAMPLE  OK
```

Our completed EXAMPLE looks like this:

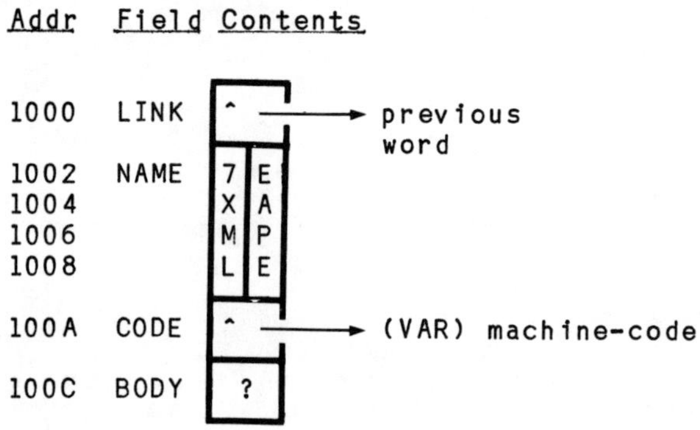

The question mark simply means that EXAMPLE is uninitialized, so the contents of its parameter field are unknown.

Constants are constructed in much the same way that variables are:

```
10 CONSTANT TEN  OK
```

Internally, TEN has these fields:

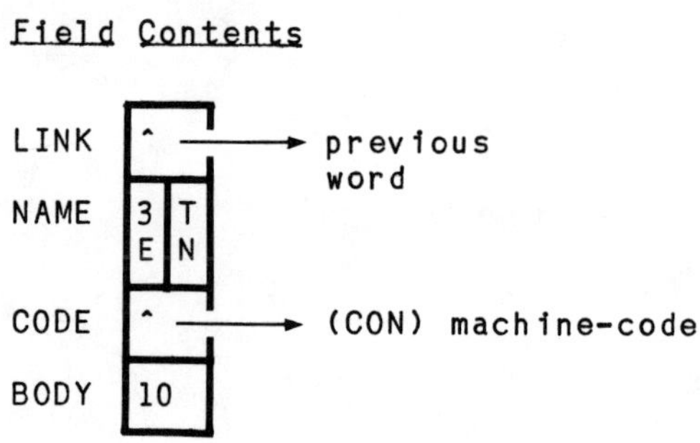

The code field points to the machine-code routine (CON), sometimes called DOCON ("do-constant"), which is the "run-time" code for a constant. All constants have this same code field. The action of (CON) is to push the value in the parameter field of a word onto the stack. (CON) then returns to FORTH at the address NEXT.

Many FORTH primitives like DUP, SWAP, and OVER are written in machine code for extra speed. For words like these, the machine code is assembled into the body of the definition. The code field, which always points to machine code, simply points to the body of the definition:

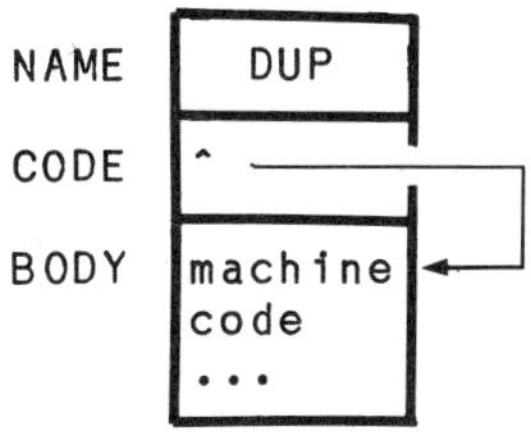

Like (VAR) and (CON), machine-code words must return to FORTH at the address NEXT.

While we have shown the link field preceding the name field and the code field preceding the parameter field, these fields can occur in any order. An experimental proposal to the Forth-83 Standard suggests the following primitives to convert one field address to another:

WORD	STACK	
>BODY	cfa -- pfa	lfa means link field address.
>NAME	cfa -- nfa	nfa means name field address.
>LINK	cfa -- lfa	cfa means code field address.
BODY>	pfa -- cfa	pfa means parameter field
NAME>	nfa -- cfa	address.
LINK>	nfa -- cfa	
N>LINK	nfa -- lfa	
L>NAME	lfa -- nfa	

How FORTH works

Colon definitions are saved in the dictionary as a sequence of compilation addresses. These addresses are stored in the body of the definition. Look closely at the following colon definitions and their accompanying diagrams:

```
: <=  ( nl n2 -- f)
\ true if nl is less than or equal to n2.
  > NOT ;

: WITHIN  ( n low high -- f)
\ true if n lies within low and high, that is,
\ low <= n < high.
  -ROT OVER <= -ROT < AND  ;
```

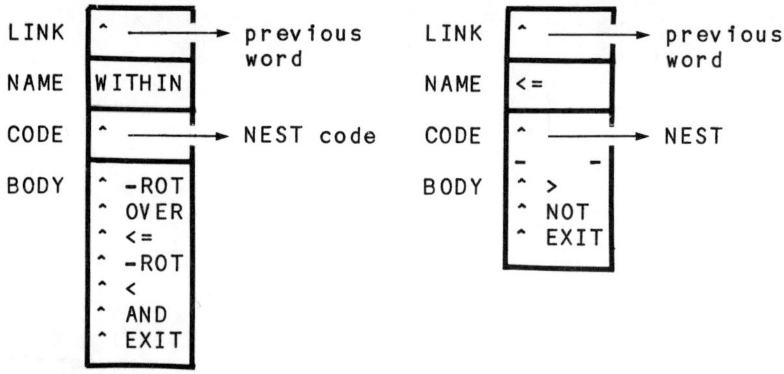

From the diagrams you can see that the code field of a colon definition points to a machine-code routine called NEST, DOCOL ("do-colon"), or something similar. The body of the definition is simply a sequence of the compilation addresses of the words which went into the definition. Notice that the final compilation address points to EXIT and not to [;]. This is the same EXIT that you studied in the flow of control chapter. It is used to exit a colon definition and return to the word that called it. In some FORTHs, this final EXIT is named UNNEST or ;S ("semi-S").

To follow the interplay between NEST, which begins a colon definition, and EXIT, which ends it, let's assume that FORTH is about to execute the OVER instruction of WITHIN:

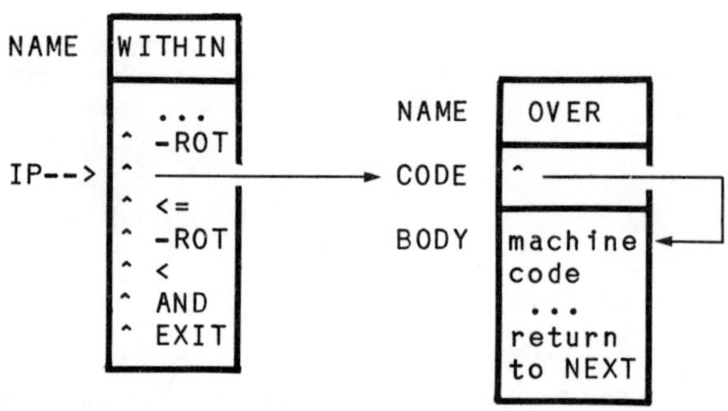

What we mean by "about to execute" is that the FORTH instruction pointer (IP) is pointing to the compilation address of OVER in the body of WITHIN. The instruction pointer itself is set and maintained by the NEXT routine. NEXT is the "inner interpreter" or "address interpreter" of the FORTH language. In a sense, NEXT is the "heart" of FORTH.

NEXT has two important jobs:

1. Execute the machine code pointed to by the compilation address pointed to by the instruction pointer.

2. Increment the instruction pointer to point to the next compilation address. By repeating these two steps, NEXT will execute all the compilation addresses in a definition.

The instruction pointer points to an address which points to machine code. This scheme of representing definitions as pointers to pointers to code makes FORTH an "indirect threaded-code" language, or ITC for short. Direct threaded-code FORTHs also exist but are less common.

In the diagram above, the compilation address of OVER is shown pointing to its code field.

> **The compilation address of a word is identical to its code-field address. This address is the normal way to refer to a word by its location.**

NEXT must increment the instruction pointer to point to the compilation address of <= either before or after it executes OVER. FORTHs which increment, then execute, are called "pre-incrementing" FORTHs. In this example, we assume that you are using a pre-incrementing FORTH. This means that while an instruction is being executed, the instruction pointer points to the next compilation address. We will use this fact to our advantage a little later in the chapter.

While OVER is being executed, the instruction pointer points to the address of <= . When OVER returns, NEXT first increments the instruction pointer to point to the address of -ROT and then executes <= :

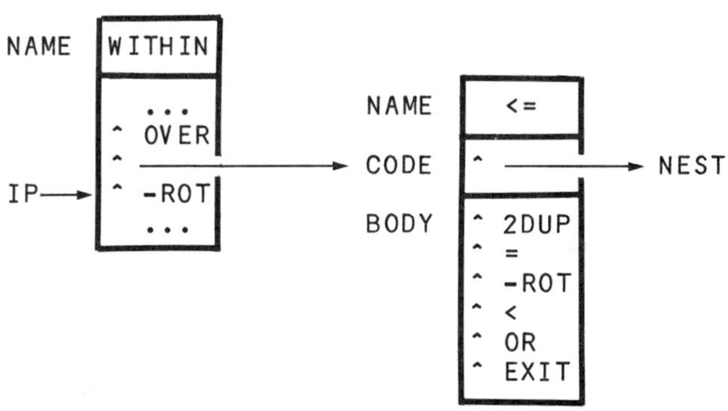

Executing <= means executing the machine code pointed to by the code field of <= --in this case, NEST. NEST pushes the current value of the instruction pointer onto the return stack and then modifies it to point to the first compilation address (that of 2DUP) in the body of <= . NEXT then continues execution at the 2DUP of <= rather than at the -ROT of WITHIN. Since we are assuming a pre-incrementing FORTH, the instruction pointer is incremented before 2DUP is executed. Our diagram now looks like this:

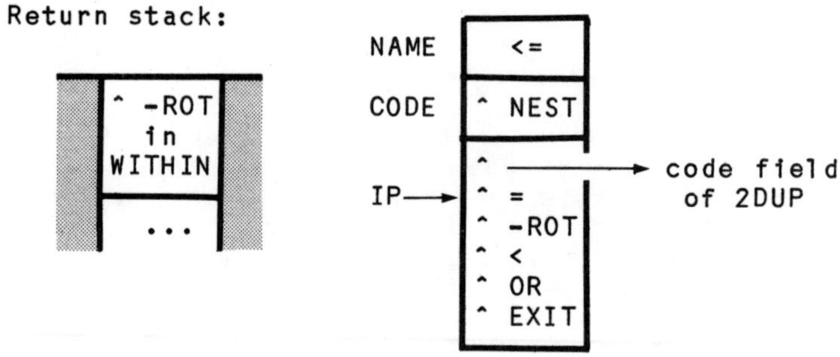

Execution continues in <= until the EXIT is reached. Just before executing EXIT, our diagram looks like this:

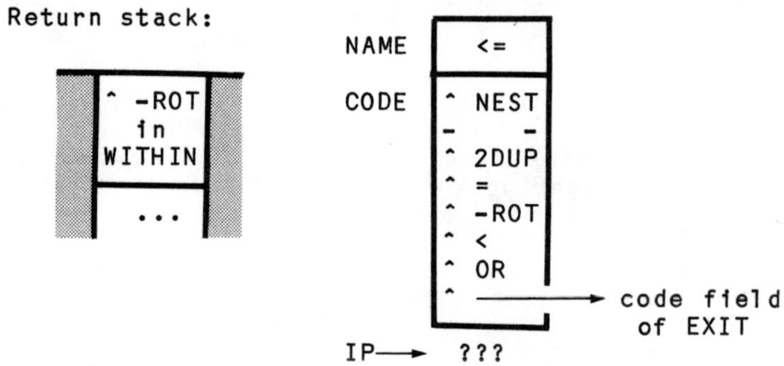

The instruction pointer points past the end of the definition and is meaningless. Fortunately, it will soon be discarded. When EXIT runs, it pops the address on top of the return stack back into the instruction pointer, effectively "returning to" that address. Execution now continues with the -ROT of WITHIN.

Eventually, the EXIT in WITHIN will run, and control will be returned to the word which called WITHIN. As each word exits in turn, control will be passed upward until it reaches the highest level of execution. This level is called the "outer interpreter" or "text interpreter." The outer interpreter, like the inner interpreter, has two important jobs:

1. Request input. The input comes either from the user at the keyboard or from mass storage. We will take a closer look at this in the next chapter.

2. Interpret each word in the input, either compiling or executing it as appropriate. By repeating these two steps indefinitely, FORTH compiles and executes all programs according to the commands given in the input.

Compiling versus interpreting

When you enter a line from the keyboard or LOAD a screen, the text interpreter immediately interprets and executes each word that it reads. This is called the "interpret state" of FORTH. On the other hand, once the interpreter begins a colon definition, it compiles the address of each word that it reads. This is the "compile state" of the language.

FORTH keeps track of which state it is in with the system variable STATE. STATE is zero while interpreting and non-zero while compiling. Let's define a word to see what state we're in:

```
: STATE?  ( --)
\ print the system state.
  STATE @
  IF   ." COMPILING"
  ELSE ." INTERPRETING"
  THEN  ;
```

Try it out from the keyboard:

```
STATE? INTERPRETING  OK
```

Now try it in a definition:

```
: TEST  STATE?  ;  OK

TEST INTERPRETING  OK
```

The STATE? in TEST is compiled and doesn't run until TEST itself is executed in the interpret state. What we need is some way of executing a word in the middle of a definition. FORTH provides the pair of words [("left-bracket") and] ("right-bracket") to let us change states at will. The [puts us in interpret state; the] returns us to compile state. They are normally used in pairs to bracket the sequence to be executed:

```
FORGET TEST  OK

: TEST  [ STATE? ]  ; INTERPRETING  OK

TEST  OK
```

This time, the bracketed STATE? runs as expected. But the brackets cause us to change states, so the message

"INTERPRETING" is printed. And because STATE? is interpreted, it is never compiled. When TEST runs, it has nothing to do.

To see the message "COMPILING," we need a STATE? that will execute while FORTH is in the compile state. We can use the command IMMEDIATE to modify a word so that it runs while compiling. IMMEDIATE must appear immediately after the definition of the word you wish to modify:

```
FORGET STATE?  OK

: STATE?  ( --)
\ print the system state.
  STATE @
  IF   ." COMPILING"
  ELSE ." INTERPRETING"
  THEN  ;

: TEST  STATE?  ; COMPILING  OK

TEST  OK
```

The immediate word STATE? now runs while compiling, leaving TEST with nothing to do.

Making a word immediate is a permanent change. If you ever need to compile an immediate word, however, you can force its compilation with the command [COMPILE]:

```
: TEST-AGAIN  [COMPILE] STATE?  ;  OK

TEST-AGAIN INTERPRETING  OK
```

Words which run while compiling are called "compiler words" and are, by definition, immediate. You have already used used compiler words like IF and THEN in flow-of-control constructs. You may even have noticed that the semicolon which ends a definition must be a compiler word, since it must run to change FORTH back to the interpret state. Furthermore, you have seen that the semicolon causes the word EXIT (or its equivalent) to be compiled at the end of the definition.

> The power of compiling words lies in their ability to substitute a low-level command sequence for a high-level compiler construct.

Literals

Compiling words let you mix data and code within the same definition. Suppose, for example, you use a number inside of a definition:

```
: FOUR+  4 +  ;
```

If FORTH were simply to compile the number 4 into the definition where it occurs, the inner interpreter would try to execute a word at compilation address 4, which is not what you mean. And yet, the logical place to save a number is inside the definition where it occurs. What we need is some way to include the number within the definition while shielding it from execution.

When the text interpreter reads the definition of FOUR+, it compiles the following sequence:

```
NAME   FOUR+

BODY   ^ (LIT)
       4
       ^ +
       ^ EXIT
```

The text interpreter adds the compilation address of (LIT) ("paren-lit"), also called DOLIT ("do-literal") or just LIT, in front of the 4. (LIT) must do two things when it runs:

1. First, it must push the number which follows it onto the stack.

2. Then it must move the instruction pointer past this number to the next compilation address.

Here is a possible definition of (LIT):

```
: (LIT)  ( -- n)
\ run-time code for a compiled number.
  R@ @        ( retrieves number)
  R> 2+ >R  ( adjusts IP)   ;
```

How does it work? Assuming a pre-incrementing FORTH, when (LIT) runs, the NEST in its code field pushes the address of the next instruction to be executed in FOUR+ onto the return stack. In this case, the return address points to the 4. The sequence R@ copies this address to the parameter stack for @ to use. Now a copy of the 4 is on the stack. The next sequence, R> 2+ >R, adds 2 to the return address, moving it past the 4. When (LIT) returns (via its EXIT), the inner interpreter will continue running FOUR+ at the [+] instruction.

The final result is that the number 4 is saved and restored "literally" as the number 4. So the literal 4 is saved "in-line," ie, mixed in with the code. Other kinds of literals can be saved in-line with the same technique. Consider, for example, the string literals from the chapter on strings. They could be compiled as follows:

```
: FELIX  ( -- string)
\ leaves the string "CAT."
  " CAT"  ;
```

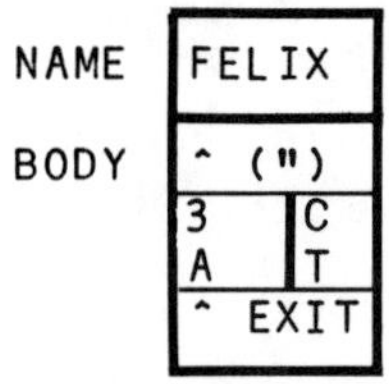


```
: (")   ( -- string)
\ run-time string literal.
  R@ COUNT   ( retrieves string)
  2DUP +     ( # bytes to skip)
  R> + >R    ( adjusts IP)  ;
```

You can make your own numeric literals with the command LITERAL. LITERAL is a compiling word which pops a number from the parameter stack and builds it into a literal. This number is usually calculated between the commands [and] just before the LITERAL. For example, another definition of FOUR+ might be as follows:

```
: FOUR+  [ 4 ] LITERAL  +  ;
```

This definition produces exactly the same code as the previous definition for FOUR+.

LITERAL is used to best advantage whenever a calculation results in a constant value. Rather than compile each step of the calculation into a definition, you can perform the calculation between [and] and save the results as a literal. This saves both computer time and memory.

Suppose you want to change the value of one word from within the definition of another. You might write something like this:

```
0 VALUE SWITCH

: TURN-ON  -1 ( TRUE)  ['] SWITCH >BODY !  ;
```

But since the address of SWITCH is constant, the expression ['] SWITCH >BODY is also constant. You can significantly improve TURN-ON like this:

```
: TURN-ON  -1  [ ' SWITCH >BODY ] LITERAL !  ;
```

> Constant expressions should be compiled as literals with the word LITERAL whenever possible.

The definition of ['] itself can be based on LITERAL:

```
: ['] ( -- addr)
\ compile an address literal.
  ' [COMPILE] LITERAL ;
 IMMEDIATE
```

Constructing compiler words

When LITERAL runs, it must compile the address of (LIT) into the word currently being defined. It must also pop a number from the stack and add it to the dictionary following (LIT). The following definition of LITERAL does all this:

```
: LITERAL  ( n --) ( -- n)
\ compiles a numeric literal.
  ['] (LIT) ,  \ add (LIT).
            ,  \ add n.
;  IMMEDIATE
```

You can see from the two stack diagrams, which specify separate compile-time and run-time actions, that compiling words are closely related to defining words.

> Compiler words are local versions of defining words for use within a definition. They specify both the in-line storage of data during compilation of a definition, and the run-time action to be performed on these data when the definition is later executed.

Since the action of adding a compilation address to the dictionary is a part of every compiling word, it has been factored out into the command COMPILE. Here is a more readable definition of LITERAL, using COMPILE:

```
: LITERAL  ( n --) ( -- n)
\ compiles a numeric literal.
  COMPILE (LIT)  \ add (LIT).
              ,  \ add n.
;  IMMEDIATE
```

The definition of COMPILE itself is relatively straightforward:

```
: COMPILE  ( --)
\ treats the following address as a
  literal and compiles it into the
  definition in progress.
  R@ @  ( retrieves the address)
  R> 2+ >R  ( skips the address)
  ,         ( compiles it)  ;
```

This definition of COMPILE is the same as the definition given for (LIT), with the addition of the comma to compile the address literal.

Here are the compiling word constructors we have learned so far:

WORD	STACK	ACTION
STATE	-- addr	System variable. A non-zero value means compile state.
[	--	Sets interpret state.
]	--	Sets compile state.
IMMEDIATE	--	Makes the latest definition immediate.
[COMPILE]	--	Adds the compilation address of name to the definition in progress, even if name is immediate. Used in a definition in the form: [COMPILE] name.
LITERAL	n -- -- n	Compiles n into the current definition. When the definition is later executed, n is pushed on the stack.
COMPILE	--	Adds the compilation address of name to the definition in progress. Used in a definition in the form: COMPILE name.
.(	.(xxx)	Prints the message xxx.

State-dumb and state-smart

All words in the Forth-83 Standard have the same action regardless of the state of the system and are therefore said to be "state-dumb." You have already seen how you must use ' outside of a definition and ['] inside of a definition to achieve the same results. And while you can use a ." to print a message from within a definition, you must use .(("dot-paren") to print a message outside of a definition:

```
.( A MESSAGE) A MESSAGE  OK
```

The word .(uses a right parenthesis as the message delimiter. While you seldom need to write yourself a message from the keyboard, you can use .(to leave a message on a screen. When you later LOAD the screen, the message will be printed.

You have also seen some words which apparently act the same way inside and outside a definition, such as ASCII and string literals. These words are "state-smart." They examine STATE and take compile-time or interpretive actions accordingly. If compiling, they compile data and a run-time action to mimic their own interpretive action when the definition being compiled is later run.

In the previous chapter on defining words, we presented a definition of IS which could be used meaningfully only outside of a definition. We used IS to set values in deferred words like SURPRISE:

```
: THING1  ." FIRST ACTION"  ;
: THING2  ." SECOND ACTION"  ;

DEFER SURPRISE
```

Now we are ready to define a state-smart version of IS:

```
: IS  ( value --)
\ sets the body of the following word to value.
\ If compiling, the word set is the one which
\ follows in the definition.
  STATE @  ( compiling?)
  IF   COMPILE (IS)  ( run-time action)
  ELSE ' >BODY !     ( interpretive action)
  THEN  ;  IMMEDIATE
```

The compile-time action of IS is to compile the word (IS) into the definition currently being defined. In this way, IS acts like a compiler word. The definition of (IS) is similar to the definition of COMPILE:

```
: (IS)  ( value --)
\ the run-time action of IS.
  R@ @  >BODY !  ( retrieves target address)
  R> 2+ >R       ( adjusts IP)  ;
```

Thus, IS works the same way inside or outside of a definition:

```
' THING1 IS SURPRISE  OK
SURPRISE FIRST ACTION  OK

: LATER  ['] THING2 IS SURPRISE  ;
SURPRISE FIRST ACTION  OK
```

Remember, IS has already run to compile (IS) in LATER, but LATER hasn't run yet:

```
LATER  OK
SURPRISE SECOND ACTION  OK
```

You could use IS to improve the definition of TURN-ON given earlier:

```
: TURN-ON  -1 IS SWITCH  ;

0 IS SWITCH  OK
SWITCH . 0  OK

TURN-ON  OK
SWITCH . -1  OK
```

Flow-of-control extension

The flow-of-control operators like IF, BEGIN, and LOOP are all compiling words. They compile in-line addresses as well as the run-time code which uses these addresses to alter the flow of control. Both the compile-time and run-time actions of all the flow-of-control operators can be reduced to a small set of primitives. The "system extension" to the Forth-83 Standard suggests the following names for these primitives:

Run-time primitives:

WORD	STACK	ACTION
BRANCH	--	unconditionally transfers control to the in-line address which follows.
?BRANCH	--	"question-branch." If the flag is false, transfers unconditionally to the address which follows, as in BRANCH; otherwise, skips this address and continues normal execution.

Compile-time primitives:

WORD	STACK	ACTION
<MARK	-- addr	"backward-mark." Marks the destination of a backward branch.
<RESOLVE	addr --	"backward-resolve." Compiles the destination address left by <MARK. This address must immediately follow a BRANCH or ?BRANCH.
>MARK	-- addr	"forward-mark." Marks the destination of a forward branch.
>RESOLVE	addr --	"forward-resolve." Calculates and compiles a destination address from the address left by <MARK. This address must immediately follow a BRANCH or ?BRANCH.

For example, the IF--ELSE--THEN operators can be defined this way:

```
: IF      COMPILE ?BRANCH   >MARK   ;  IMMEDIATE

: ELSE    COMPILE BRANCH    >MARK
          2SWAP  >RESOLVE   ;  IMMEDIATE

: THEN    >RESOLVE          ;  IMMEDIATE
```

Here is a definition of MAX using IF--THEN along with its internal diagram:

```
: MAX   2DUP < IF SWAP THEN  DROP  ;
```

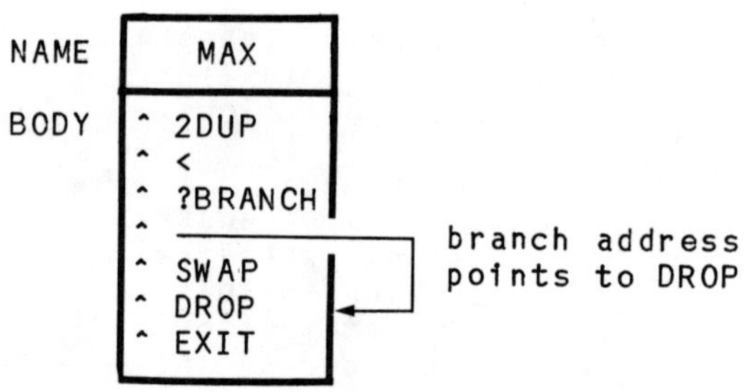

Some FORTHs use a "branch" address which is relative to the instruction pointer; others use the destination memory address.

It is also possible to design new flow-of-control constructs based directly on the current operators. For example, if your FORTH doesn't support ?DO, you can add it this way:

```
: ?DO   COMPILE 2DUP  COMPILE =
        [COMPILE] IF    COMPILE 2DROP
        [COMPILE] ELSE  [COMPILE] DO   ;
 IMMEDIATE

:  DO   COMPILE TRUE  ( -1 CONSTANT TRUE)
        [COMPILE] IF    [COMPILE] DO   ;
 IMMEDIATE

: LOOP  [COMPILE] LOOP  [COMPILE] THEN  ;
 IMMEDIATE

: +LOOP [COMPILE] +LOOP [COMPILE] THEN  ;
 IMMEDIATE
```

This automatically converts any ?DO--LOOP construct into this one:

```
... 2DUP = IF 2DROP ELSE DO ... LOOP THEN ...
```

DO--LOOP constructs are converted this way:

```
... TRUE IF DO ... LOOP THEN ...
```

Exercises

1. Define the word DLITERAL, which acts like LITERAL but which saves and restores double numbers.

2. The construct

```
... flag IF LEAVE THEN ...
```

is commonly found in DO--LOOPs. Write the word ?LEAVE to replace it:

```
... flag ?LEAVE ...
```

3. Design a new compiler word which allows in-line vectored execution. Use the word SELECT to begin a series of words and the word COMPLETE to end them. The run-time action of the SELECT--COMPLETE series is to use the number on top of the stack as an index into the series. The word selected by the index is executed, and control then continues with the word following COMPLETE:

```
: ZERO  ." FIRST "  ;  : ONE    ." SECOND "  ;
: TWO   ." THIRD "  ;  : THREE  ." FOURTH "  ;

: SELECTIVE  ( n --)
  SELECT  ZERO ONE TWO THREE  COMPLETE
  ." ACTION"  ;

0 SELECTIVE FIRST ACTION  OK
2 SELECTIVE THIRD ACTION  OK
```

4. Write the word BODY-OF which leaves the parameter address of the word which follows on the stack. Make BODY-OF state-smart, so it works both inside and outside of definitions:

```
12 VALUE DOZEN

: BAKER'S-DOZEN  ( --)
  13 BODY-OF DOZEN !  ;

BODY-OF DOZEN ? 12  OK
BAKER'S-DOZEN  OK
BODY-OF DOZEN ? 13  OK
```

13 The input stream and mass storage

The text interpreter reads and operates on each word of input until the input "stream" is exhausted and then asks for more. Input normally comes from the lines you type in at the keyboard, unless you choose to LOAD a screen or a range of screens. We will use the term "input stream" to mean the input to the text interpreter, no matter where it is coming from.

The input stream

The text interpreter determines the source of the input stream by examining the system variable BLK ("b-l-k"). If the value of BLK is zero, it takes its input from the terminal input buffer (TIB). Otherwise, it uses the value of BLK as a block number and takes its input from that block. This is why you can never LOAD block number zero.

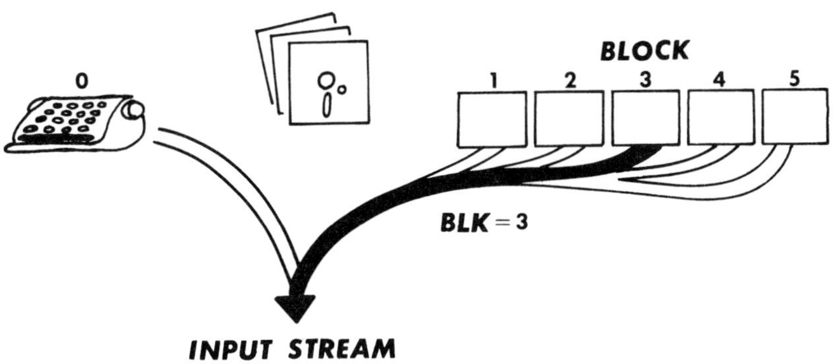

Since the input stream comes from either TIB or from a block, it will always be read from memory. You can think of the input stream as an array or string of characters whose starting address and length can be determined by the following word:

```
: SOURCE  ( -- addr length)
\ determines the starting address and length in bytes
\ of the input stream.
  BLK @ ?DUP  ( from BLOCK ?)
  IF  BLOCK 1024  ELSE  TIB #TIB @  THEN  ;
```

The text interpreter uses the system variable >IN ("to-in") to keep track of where it is in the input stream. As it reads each word, it advances the index >IN to point to the next position to be read. This address and the number of characters remaining to be read is given by the expression:

```
SOURCE >IN @ /STRING
```

(At this point, you may wish to review /STRING in the chapter on strings.)

When the index in >IN is equal to the length of the input stream, there are no more characters to be read. The input stream is said to be "exhausted," and the text interpreter will request further input. The word STOP takes advantage of this to immediately terminate a LOAD whenever it is executed from within a block. STOP fools the text interpreter into thinking that the block has already been read:

```
: STOP  ( --)
\ stops a LOAD immediately.
  1024 >IN !  ;
```

The word MANY works from the keyboard in a similar way; it causes the commands in the line just typed to be repeated until a key is pressed:

```
: MANY  ( --)
\ re-execute the commands in the line just typed.
  KEY? NOT  IF  0 >IN !  THEN  ;

CR .( AGAIN!) MANY
AGAIN!
AGAIN!
AGAIN!
( key pressed here)  OK
```

Be sure you understand why MANY must appear on the same line as the commands you want to repeat.

The command WORD

You can use the command WORD to read the input stream. WORD uses the character on the top of the stack as a delimiter and reads the input stream up to the delimiter into a temporary packed string, returning the address of the string. Here is a simple word which simply reads and types the next word in the input stream:

```
: WHAT?  ( --)
\ reads and types the next word in the input stream.
  BL ( delimiter) WORD  COUNT TYPE  ;

CLEAR  OK
1 2 3 WHAT? OVER .S OVER
STACK: 1 2 3  OK
```

The OVER is read by WHAT? instead of by the text interpreter and so is never executed.

If the input stream is exhausted while it is being read, WORD returns with a string of whatever characters were available. If WORD is called when the input stream is already exhausted, this string has a length of zero:

```
CR . . . WHAT?
3 2 1  OK
```

The text interpreter itself uses WORD (or something similar) to read each word in the input stream. It then uses FIND to find the word in the dictionary from the packed name returned by WORD. FIND has a curious syntax which largely reflects the needs of the text interpreter:

WORD	STACK	ACTION
WORD	delim -- ^string	Returns the address of a packed string read from the input stream up to the delimiter or until the input is exhausted. Skips leading delimiters. The packed string is followed by a blank not included in the count. If more than 255 characters are read, the count is meaningless.
FIND	^string --	Finds the packed name at ^string in the dictionary.
	-- ^string 0	If the name is not found, returns ^string and false.
	-- cfa flag	If the name is found, returns the compilation address (cfa) and a flag with one of two values: 1 means the word is IMMEDIATE; -1 means the word is not IMMEDIATE.

The text interpreter uses a sequence like BL WORD FIND to find a word in the dictionary. The word ASCII can also be based on WORD:

```
: ASCII  ( -- n)
\ used in the form: ASCII c
\ where c follows in the input stream.
\ Returns the 7-bit ASCII code of c.
  BL WORD 1+ C@  ( read the next char)
  STATE @  ( ASCII is state-smart!)
  IF  [COMPILE] LITERAL  THEN  ;
   IMMEDIATE
```

WORD skips leading delimiters:

```
ASCII              A . 65  OK
```

This can lead to some unfortunate situations. Consider, for example, this definition of `.(` :

```
: .(  ( --)
\ reads and TYPEs text up to the next ")".
  ASCII ) ( delimiter) WORD  COUNT TYPE  ;
```

The following message prints correctly:

```
.( PRINT ME) PRINT ME OK
```

But when the message is empty, strange things may happen:

```
.( )( IGNORE ME) ( IGNORE ME OK
```

What happens? When the text interpreter reads the `.(` , it leaves the index in >IN pointing just past the blank delimiter to the next right parenthesis. When `.(` is executed, WORD treats this right parenthesis as a leading delimiter and ignores it. WORD then reads the input up to the next right parenthesis into a packed string--which `.(` then prints.

This problem often occurs in words which use WORD to read the input stream with a non-blank delimiter. Such words should be based on PARSE rather than on WORD:

```
: PARSE  ( delimiter -- string)
\ works like WORD, but doesn't ignore
\ leading delimiters.
  SOURCE >IN @ /STRING
  >R C@ OVER =  ( peek at next char, if any)
  R> 0> AND     ( does it equal delimiter?)
  IF  DROP 0 PAD !  ( build empty string)
      1 >IN +!  PAD EXIT
  THEN  WORD COUNT  ;
```

Both `.(` and `(` can now be safely defined with PARSE:

```
: (   ( --)
\ reads and ignores text up to the next ")".
  ASCII ) ( delimiter) PARSE 2DROP  ;
 IMMEDIATE

: .(   ( --)
\ reads and TYPEs text up to the next ")".
  ASCII ) ( delimiter) PARSE  TYPE  ;
```

String literals can be implemented with PARSE and the run-time word (") from the chapter on compiler words. Here is a simple version which doesn't allow imbedded double-quotes:

```
: (")   ( -- string)
\ run-time string literal.
  R@ COUNT  2DUP +  R> + >R  ;
```

```
: "   ( -- string)
\ generates string literals.
  ASCII " PARSE
  PAD SWAP CPACK PAD COUNT
  STATE @
  IF  COMPILE (")
      HERE OVER 1+ ALLOT
      SWAP CPACK
  THEN  ;  IMMEDIATE
```

Conditional compilation

Some applications may need to run in several different environments. For example, words which control a printer may need to change with each new printer. While it is possible to write one word which controls several printers, it is more efficient to write one word for each printer. Once a printer is selected, only the word controlling that printer should be compiled.

One approach you might take to implement selective or "conditional" compilation is to put definitions onto separate screens in a file. You can then write a word which tests a condition and compiles the appropriate screen. The word might contain a code sequence like this:

```
... ( condition is on the stack)
DUP 1 =  IF     8 LOAD  ELSE
DUP 2 =  IF   9 10 THRU  ELSE
    ( otherwise:)
DROP            11 LOAD
THEN THEN
...
```

It would be nice if this sequence could appear in interpret mode. Unfortunately, the IF--ELSE--THEN construct is compile-only and must appear within the body of a definition. Therefore, you must invent a name and compile the code sequence into its definition. Furthermore, since the new definition will be LOADing the screens, it will precede any definitions on these screens in the dictionary and so cannot be "forgotten" after the LOAD.

Alternately, you can design a class of "smart comments" for conditional code. These comments normally act like ordinary comments--any code they contain is ignored. But under certain conditions, smart comments "disappear" and the code they contain is read and processed by the text interpreter:

```
VARIABLE CHOOSE  ( smart comment selector)

: (1  ( --)
\ the lefthand side of smart comment class 1.
\ If CHOOSE isn't 1, the code in the comment is
\ ignored.
  CHOOSE @ 1 <> IF  ASCII ) PARSE  2DROP THEN  ;
 IMMEDIATE

: (2  ( --)
\ the lefthand side of smart comment class 2.
  CHOOSE @ 2 <> IF  ASCII ) PARSE  2DROP THEN  ;
 IMMEDIATE

: )  ( --)
\ the righthand side of a smart comment.
;  IMMEDIATE
```

The dummy definition of `)` is necessary because when a smart comment is selected, all words included in the comment will be processed by the text interpreter, including the trailing `)`. For this same reason, the `)` must be preceded and followed by at least one blank.

Here is a smart comment in action:

```
2 CHOOSE ! OK

(1 : HI ." HELLO" ; ) (2 : HI ." BONJOUR" ; )  OK
CR HI
BONJOUR OK
```

Handy hints

You can use smart comments for debugging, too! Surround all your debugging code, inside or outside of definitions, with smart comments. Once your program is working, you can make the debugging code "disappear." If you later need to change the program again, the debugging code is immediately available.

Mass storage

In the chapter on the editor you learned how to copy text from one screen to another a line at a time. You can copy entire screens at a time by moving text directly from one block to another. For example, suppose you want to copy screen 2 to screen 4. If you could find the address of the buffers holding these screens in memory, you could CMOVE all 1024 bytes from one screen to the other.

The word BLOCK reads a block into a memory buffer and returns the starting address of that buffer. BLOCK, in essence, is a 1024-byte window into a file. Words like LIST, LOAD, and even the editor itself are based on BLOCK (or a word very much like it). You might expect the following sequence to copy screen 2 to screen 4:

```
2 BLOCK 4 BLOCK 1024 CMOVE
```

The 2 BLOCK reads block 2 into a buffer in memory and returns its address. The 4 BLOCK returns the buffer address of block 4. You now have the "from" address, "to" address, and number of bytes to move--the three arguments required by CMOVE.

Unfortunately, you have no control over which buffer is selected by BLOCK. It could happen that block 4 is read into the same buffer as block 2, in which case you copy block 4 to block 4, which is not what you meant. You can solve this problem by using a third intermediate buffer in memory:

```
2 BLOCK PAD 1024 CMOVE  PAD 4 BLOCK 1024 CMOVE
```

Here, PAD is used as the intermediate buffer.

PAD is only guaranteed to be 84 characters long, but on most FORTHs, it is much larger. If PAD is smaller than 1024 bytes on your system, substitute a suitable memory array:

```
CREATE TEMP-BUF  1024 ALLOT
```

Once screen 2 has been copied, you must tell FORTH that block 4 has been changed and needs to be (eventually) rewritten to mass storage. You can do this with the word UPDATE. UPDATE marks the most recently read BLOCK as updated or changed. (If you were in the editor, it would automatically UPDATE a screen when you changed its contents.) The complete sequence for copying screen 2 to screen 4 is:

```
2 BLOCK PAD 1024 CMOVE  PAD 4 BLOCK 1024 CMOVE UPDATE
```

Now that you know how to copy one screen to another, you can write a utility to copy a range of screens the same way:

```
: SCOPY  ( n1 n2 n3 --)
\ copies n3 blocks from block n1 to block n2.
  >R  2DUP <  ( moving upward?)
  IF  0 R> 1-
     ?DO OVER I + BLOCK PAD 1024 CMOVE
         PAD OVER I + BLOCK 1024 CMOVE UPDATE
         -1
     +LOOP
  ELSE  R> 0
     ?DO OVER I + BLOCK PAD 1024 CMOVE
         PAD OVER I + BLOCK 1024 CMOVE UPDATE
      LOOP
  THEN  2DROP  ;
```

The Forth-83 Standard also provides the word BUFFER which, like BLOCK, selects an available buffer and returns its memory address. Unlike BLOCK, however, the block number is "assigned to" the buffer and is not necessarily read into it from mass storage. BUFFER is designed for operating systems that require you to write a block before reading it for the first time. You can initialize a block this way:

```
10 BUFFER  1024 BL FILL  UPDATE
```

Block 10 is created and initialized to blanks.

Reading blocks

You now have all the words you need to write the INDEX function described in the chapter on the editor. INDEX reads a range of screens and types out any line that begins in the leftmost column (column 0):

```
: INDEX  ( from-block# to-block# --)
\ prints any line that begins in column 0.
  1+ SWAP               ( read each block)
  DO I BLOCK  1024 0    ( read each line)
     DO  DUP I + C@ BL <>  ( column 0 not blank?)
        IF  CR  DUP I + 64 TYPE  THEN
        64 ( next line is 64 bytes away)
    +LOOP  DROP
  LOOP  ;
```

If you use INDEX on screen 2 of the SAMPLE file, you will see:

```
2 2 INDEX
\ Somewhat trickier words.
: TRICKY  ( start# -- end#)
\ Starting equals ending number.
: TRICK2  ( start# -- end#)
\ The answer is always three.
```

Virtual arrays

In writing INDEX, we took advantage of the fact that screens are exact multiples of lines, that is, there are exactly 16 lines per screen. This means that no line starts on one block and "crosses over" into the next block. So if a screen is brought into memory with BLOCK, all the lines on that screen are in memory too.

The lines on a screen spend most of their time in mass storage, and are brought into memory on demand. You could say that they exist in a "virtual" memory. As such, they don't take up valuable main memory space. In FORTH, virtual memory arrays are easy to implement, provided that the array fits entirely within a block. Here is a defining word which creates virtual arrays 1024 bytes (512 cells) long:

```
: VIRTUAL-ARRAY
  CREATE ,    ( block# --)
  DOES>       ( -- addr)
    @ BLOCK  ;
```

Notice that no ALLOT is necessary. Before you create a virtual array, you must decide which block to use:

```
4 VIRTUAL-ARRAY HOLD-IT  OK
```

Block 4 of the active file is assigned to HOLD-IT. Use SAMPLE to make the sample file active, then save a string in HOLD-IT:

```
SAMPLE  OK

" TRUST ME" HOLD-IT SWAP CPACK  UPDATE  OK
```

The UPDATE is necessary to ensure that HOLD-IT will be rewritten to mass storage when the file is closed:

```
FLUSH  OK
SAMPLE  OK

CR HOLD-IT COUNT TYPE
TRUST ME  OK
```

No UPDATE is necessary here, since you are only reading HOLD-IT. UPDATE can be included in the defining word VIRTUAL-ARRAY itself, right after BLOCK.

A simple data base manager

In a simple data base manager, information is saved to and retrieved from mass storage in units called "records." A record is typically subdivided into "fields" of numbers and text. For example, in a mailing list program, the records are the addresses themselves and the fields are the name, street number, city, state, zip code, and so on.

If the record size is fixed (unvarying) and evenly divides a block (1024 bytes), then the block location of a record in a file can be found by multiplying the record number by the record size (in bytes) and then dividing the product by 1024. The remainder of this division is the byte offset of the record within the block. If the records begin on a block other than block 0, you will need to add a constant offset to the block location.

Once the block location and byte offset of a record are known, the record and all fields in it can be treated as virtual memory arrays. Here's how to find the starting address of a record:

```
  4 CONSTANT FIRST-BLOCK  ( records start here)
128 CONSTANT RECORD-SIZE  ( 8 records per block)
```

```
: RECORD  ( record# -- addr)
\ determines the starting address of a virtual
\ record.
  RECORD-SIZE *
  1024 /MOD  FIRST-BLOCK +  ( offset block#)
  BLOCK +  UPDATE  ;
```

Given the starting address, you can find all other fields just by adding an appropriate offset. You can even create the defining word FIELD to do this for you:

```
VARIABLE RECORD#  ( number of current record)

: FIELD
\ returns the address of a field in the current
\ record.  A field is defined by its offset in
\ the record.
  CREATE  ,     ( record-offset --)
  DOES>         ( -- addr)
    @  RECORD# @ RECORD +  ;

 0 FIELD NAME     ( 20-byte name field)
20 FIELD STREET   ( 30-byte street field)
50 FIELD ZIP      (  9-byte zip code field)
```

Using the string operators from the chapter on strings, you can write a word which prompts the user for name, address, and zip code and uses this information to initialize a record:

```
CREATE BUF  4 ALLOT  ( temporary buffer)

: SELECT-IT  ( --)
\ selects a record and makes it current.
  CR ." USE WHICH RECORD? "
  BUF 4 EXPECT   ( assume a valid number:)
  BUF SPAN @ VAL ( dn flag)
  2DROP ( includes D>S) RECORD# !  ;

: READ-IT  ( field-addr #bytes --)
\ reads and packs a field.
  OVER 1+ SWAP 1- EXPECT
  DUP  1+ SWAP SPAN @ CPACK  ;

: FILE-IT  ( --)
\ requests and files name, address, and zip.
  SELECT-IT  ( choose a record)
  CR ."   NAME: "    NAME 19 READ-IT
  CR ." STREET: "  STREET 29 READ-IT
  CR ."    ZIP: "     ZIP  9 READ-IT
```

Finally, PRINT-IT lets you see what's in a record:

```
: PRINT-IT  ( --)
\ prints requested record.
  SELECT-IT  ( choose a record)
  CR ."   NAME: "    NAME COUNT TYPE
  CR ." STREET: "  STREET COUNT TYPE
  CR ."    ZIP: "     ZIP COUNT TYPE  ;
```

WORD	STACK	ACTION
BLK	-- addr	Variable which selects a block number for input. If BLK is zero, input is taken from the terminal input buffer (TIB).
>IN	-- addr	Variable which contains the current offset of the input stream.
BLOCK	n -- addr	Reads block n from the active file into a memory buffer and returns the address of that buffer.
BUFFER	n -- addr	Assigns block n to a memory buffer and returns the address of that buffer. Block n may not be read from the active file into that buffer.
UPDATE	--	Marks the most recently read block for eventual rewriting to mass storage.

File extensions

When we introduced the file SAMPLE in the editor chapter, we assumed that files were available from the operating system and could be selected for editing, LISTing, and LOADing. In fact, FORTH often runs in environments which have no operating systems or files. In cases like these, FORTH itself serves as the operating system. The mass storage device, if any, is seen as one large file. Since this file is fixed in size and is always available, there is no need for words like MORE or even SAMPLE.

If files are available, however, FORTH can be extended to take advantage of them. We will present here a set of typical file commands, chosen to conform to those described in Kernighan and Plauger's Software Tools in Pascal (Addison-Wesley, 1981), but with a syntax suitably modified for the FORTH language.

You can request the use of a file from the operating system with the command OPEN. Its syntax is as follows:

```
OPEN ( name-string mode -- file-descriptor)
```

The file name follows the conventions of the operating system and may include password, device name, directory path, or whatever other options the system offers. "Mode" refers to how you wish to use the file. The two parts of a mode are the access method and the file type. Three access methods are:

Access	Definition
READ	Read file only.
WRITE	Write file only.
MODIFY	Read or write file.

Three common file types are:

Type	Definition
SCREENS	Contains ASCII characters organized into screens of 1024 bytes.
TEXT	Contains lines of text. Each line is terminated by an end-of-line character or sequence of characters. The last line of text is followed by an end-of-file character.
DATA	Contains data.

Access method and file type are added together to form the mode. For example, to open the file "SECRET" as read-only text file use this command sequence:

```
" SECRET" READ TEXT + OPEN
```

A missing access method is assumed to be MODIFY and a missing type is assumed to be SCREENS. Therefore, a mode of 0 defaults to SCREENS + MODIFY, which is the mode expected by the editor.

A file of the given name must already exist at the time it is opened. To create a new file, use MAKE. MAKE has a syntax similar to OPEN:

```
MAKE ( name-string mode -- file-descriptor)
```

If a file of this name already exists, MAKE deletes the old one and makes a new empty file.

The file descriptor returned by OPEN or MAKE is used to identify the file to other file operators. If for any reason OPEN fails to find the file or MAKE fails to create it, the file descriptor returned will be zero. File descriptors are numbers and so can be manipulated and stored like any number.

It is possible to OPEN or MAKE several files in the same program, but only one of them can be "active" at a time. The active file is the one used by BLOCK (and all words based on BLOCK). To make a file active, store its file descriptor (or a copy of it) in the value DEFAULT. The word ACTIVE makes this selection more readable:

```
: ACTIVE  ( file-descriptor --)
\ makes a file active.
  IS DEFAULT  ;

" SAMPLE" MODIFY SCREENS + OPEN ACTIVE  OK
```

The word FILE combines these operations to open a screen file and make it active:

```
: FILE  ( name-string --)
\ opens a file and makes it active.
\ Mode defaults to MODIFY SCREENS.
  0 OPEN ACTIVE  ;
```

The word SAMPLE is now easily defined:

```
: SAMPLE  ( --)
  " SAMPLE" FILE  ;
```

When you are finished with a file, you can return it to the operating system with the command CLOSE. CLOSE needs the file descriptor of the file you wish closed:

```
CLOSE  ( file-descriptor --)
```

When you close a file, the operating system updates the mass storage directory to include any changes you have made in the file. FLUSH simply closes all open files.

Here is a word which opens a file, LOADs block 1, and then closes the file:

```
: INCLUDE  ( name-string --)
\ LOADs a file by name.
  DEFAULT >R  FILE
    1 LOAD  DEFAULT CLOSE
  R> IS DEFAULT  ;
```

Block 1 can contain other LOAD block commands. Suppose, for example, you have a file which builds a random number generator. You can include this generator in a program by requesting it with INCLUDE:

```
" RANDOM NUMBER GENERATOR" INCLUDE
```

Before INCLUDE opens the file, it pushes the current file descriptor onto the return stack and restores it to DEFAULT when it's done. This lets you nest INCLUDEs, so one file can INCLUDE several more.

The final file command we will describe is DELETE. DELETE deletes a file from the mass storage directory by name:

```
DELETE  ( name-string --)
```

In addition, many operating systems let you rename files, limit their access, verify their contents, and so on. Your FORTH probably reflects these operations with words with the same name as those used by the operating system.

The CATALOG or DIRECTORY command you learned in the chapter on the editor is an example of this.

WORD	STACK	ACTION
OPEN	name-string mode -- fd	Opens a file by name. Returns file descriptor fd. File must already exist. See text for a description of mode.
MAKE	name-string mode -- fd	Creates a file by name. Returns file descriptor fd. If file already exists, it is recreated.
CLOSE	fd --	Closes a file.
DELETE	name-string --	Deletes a file by name.
DEFAULT	-- fd	Value containing the active file descriptor .
ACTIVE	fd --	Selects a file as active.
FILE	name-string --	Opens a file and makes it active. File is opened as MODIFY SCREENS.
INCLUDE	name-string --	Opens a file, LOADs block 1, then closes the file.

Exercises

1. Define the word CONTROL which, like ASCII, reads the character that follows it in the input stream, converting it to the appropriate control character:

```
HEX CONTROL X . 18 OK
```

2. Using the word IN from the exercises in the chapter on strings, write the word SEARCH. It searches a range of screens for a match with a given string pattern, printing each line that contains a match. Assuming the file SAMPLE is active, SEARCHing for a colon gives the following results:

```
" :" 1 2 SEARCH
: SIMPLE
: TRICKY ( start# -- end#)
: TRICK2 ( start# -- end#)
```

3. Write a version of RECORD which reads records into a memory buffer that you provide. The records can be any size less than 1024 bytes, but all records must be the same size. This means that a record can start on one block and end on another. By reading the record into a memory buffer, you are then able to access the fields with CMOVE. The syntax of the new RECORD is as follows:

```
RECORD ( record# buffer-address --)
```

4. Modify the simple mailing list program to include city and state fields. Change ZIP from a 9-byte text field to a 4-byte double-number field. You will also need to modify PRINT-IT to print the new information.

For advanced students:

5. Write a version of " that allows for imbedded double-quote marks:

```
CR " ""HELLO,"" IT SAID." TYPE
"HELLO," IT SAID.
```

14 Advanced topics

Vocabularies

Vocabularies are miniature dictionaries of words related to each other by function. A FORTH system typically has at least three vocabularies:

Vocabulary	Function
FORTH	This is the primary vocabulary and contains the required words of the FORTH language like DUP, SWAP, and so forth.
EDITOR	This vocabulary holds the words used by the screen editor, like <CRIGHT> and <DONE>.
ASSEMBLER	This vocabulary holds the words which generate machine code.

When you use WORDS to examine the dictionary, you first see the words in the most recently activated vocabulary, followed by the words in any other active vocabularies in their order of activation. This order is called the "search order" and is the same order used by the text interpreter when it searches for a word in the dictionary.

There are two important advantages to grouping words into vocabularies:

Speed. Words in an inactive vocabulary are not part of the search order and will not be searched by the text interpreter. For example, if you are not editing a screen, there is normally no need to search for words in the EDITOR vocabulary.

Duplicate names. You can use the same name to mean different things in different vocabularies. For example, the word FILL in the vocabulary FORTH is used to fill a memory area with a character. You might also use it within a vocabulary of process-control words to fill a tank with fluid. The text interpreter will use whichever FILL it finds in the dictionary first. Since the most recently activated vocabulary is the one searched first, it is called the "context" vocabulary.

When you first run the FORTH language, the context vocabulary is set to FORTH:

```
CREATE MARKER  OK

WORDS
MARKER
...
EDITOR
...
ASSEMBLER
...
FORTH
...
```

To activate a vocabulary, thereby making it the context vocabulary, simply execute it:

```
EDITOR  OK

WORDS
...
<DONE>
...
<CRIGHT>
...
MARKER
...
```

When the vocabulary FORTH runs, it replaces EDITOR as the context vocabulary:

```
FORTH OK

WORDS
MARKER
...
```

Some Forth-83 Standard words behave differently than their FIG-FORTH counterparts do. We can put these words in a separate vocabulary--let's call it FIG. This effectively gives us the same word with two different actions, depending on whether the context is FORTH or FIG-FORTH. Creating the vocabulary FIG is easy:

```
VOCABULARY FIG  OK
WORDS
FIG
MARKER
...
```

Now that FIG exists, you can make it the context vocabulary:

```
FIG  OK
```

Since FIG has no words of its own yet, nothing has been added to the search order. The vocabulary FIG itself is actually a word in the FORTH vocabulary. To enter new definitions into FIG, you must first make it into the "current" vocabulary with the command DEFINITIONS:

```
FIG DEFINITIONS  OK
```

DEFINITIONS simply makes the context vocabulary, which is the first searched, into the current vocabulary, which holds new words. Here are some words for the FIG vocabulary:

```
: VARIABLE  ( n --) ( -- addr)
\ takes its initial value from the stack.
  CREATE  ,  ;

10 VARIABLE DELTA

: PICK  ( .... index -- ... indexed-item)
\ works like Forth-83 PICK,
\ but counts the top item as number one.
  1- PICK  ( defined in terms of Forth-83 PICK)  ;

WORDS
PICK
DELTA
VARIABLE
```

FORTH uses the system variables CONTEXT and CURRENT to keep track of context and current vocabularies, respectively. Several words in FORTH affect the context and current vocabularies:

WORD	ACTION
<Vocabulary>	Makes itself the context vocabulary when it runs.
DEFINITIONS	Makes context into current.
:	Makes current into context.

> Be aware that any colon definition can change your vocabulary.

Different FORTHs have different ways of linking vocabularies into a search order. The Forth-83 Standard proposes using a vocabulary stack. Before we push FIG onto this stack, let's clear it:

```
ONLY  OK
```

ONLY is a smart vocabulary with the side effect of clearing all vocabularies (including FORTH) from the search order. ONLY then becomes the context vocabulary.

```
1 2 3 DUP
DUP ?
```

Even DUP is unknown, since it cannot be found in the search order.

ONLY itself has only about a dozen words. Fortunately, one of them is WORDS, so you can see the words in ONLY (try it!). Another word in ONLY is ORDER, which prints the search order from left to right, starting with context. In ORDER and diagram form, the vocabulary stack now looks like this:

```
ORDER
CONTEXT: ONLY ONLY
CURRENT: FIG
```

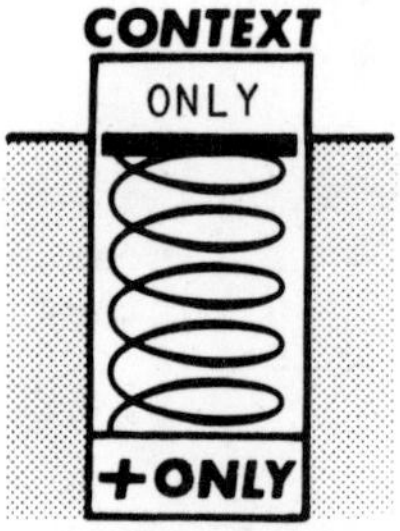

While ONLY seems to be present twice, it actually isn't on the vocabulary stack at all! The ONLY in CONTEXT is "transient." Like all context vocabularies, it is replaced when the next vocabulary runs:

```
FORTH DEFINITIONS  OK

ORDER
CONTEXT: FORTH ONLY
CURRENT: FORTH
```

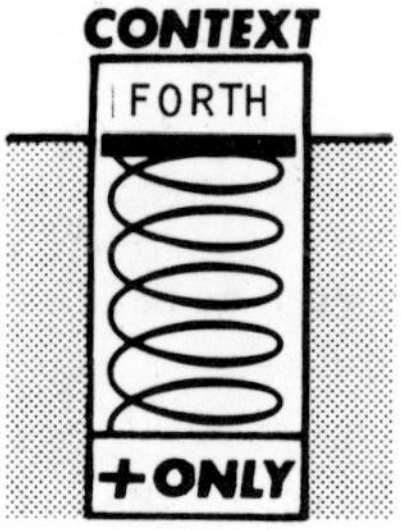

Now FORTH is the transient or context vocabulary. To make a vocabulary a permanent part of the search order ("resident"), push it onto the vocabulary stack with ALSO, which pushes the context vocabulary onto the vocabulary stack:

```
ALSO  OK

ORDER
CONTEXT: FORTH FORTH ONLY
CURRENT: FORTH
```

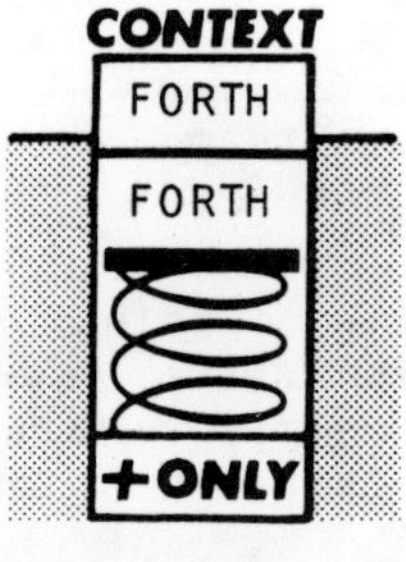

There is no way to pop an item from the vocabulary stack, but. you can always clear it with ONLY and start over. The normal search order is the one we have presented:

```
ONLY FORTH DEFINITIONS ALSO
```

FORTHs which use vocabulary stacks are usually optimized so that if the same vocabulary appears twice in the search order, it is only searched once.

You can extend the search order as needed with ALSO:

```
EDITOR ALSO FIG
ORDER
CONTEXT: FIG EDITOR FORTH ONLY
CURRENT: FORTH
```

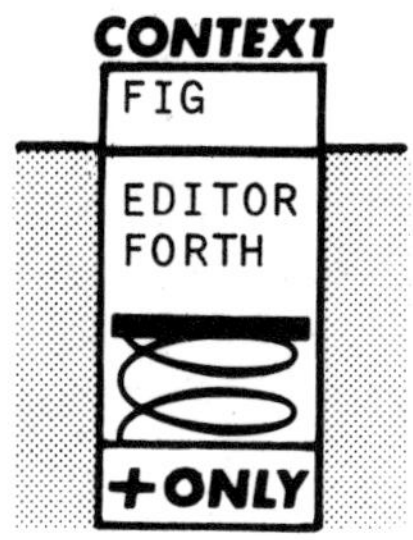

The search order is FIG, then EDITOR, then FORTH, then ONLY. The ONLY vocabulary sits "below" the stack and is not part of it.

> **The ONLY vocabulary is always searched and is usually searched last.**

The command SEAL is the one exception to this rule. SEAL deletes all occurrences of ONLY from the search order. SEAL is used in practical programming to limit the user strictly to those commands which are found in the application vocabularies.

WORD	ACTION
CONTEXT	A variable which determines the vocabulary to be searched first.
CURRENT	A variable which determines the vocabulary into which new words are to be compiled.
ONLY	Clears the vocabulary stack and makes ONLY the context vocabulary.
FORTH	The primary vocabulary.
ALSO	Pushes the context vocabulary onto the vocabulary stack.
ORDER	Prints the search order.
DEFINITIONS	Selects the context vocabulary as the current vocabulary.
SEAL	Deletes all occurrences of ONLY from the search order.

Exceptional conditions

When an error occurs for which FORTH has no reasonable course of action, it "aborts" and returns to you with an error message. Aborting a program means that FORTH immediately stops whatever it is doing and returns to the normal keyboard interpret mode. You can force a program to abort with the words ABORT or QUIT:

WORD	ACTION
ABORT	Clears the data stack and performs QUIT.
QUIT	Clears the return stack, sets interpret state, and returns you to the keyboard.

QUIT is normally used to end a program. In the CRAPS program presented in the chapter on loops, for example, when you determine that the game is won or lost, you can QUIT the program without having to return through several layers of execution.

ABORT is more commonly used when you detect an error but are unable to take corrective action. Consider this definition of ['] :

```
: '  ( -- addr)
\ returns the compilation address of the next
\ word in the input stream.
  BL WORD FIND  ( addr flag)
  0= IF ." MISSING" ABORT  THEN  ;

' GORF MISSING
```

If the word you are looking for isn't in the dictionary, ['] informs you that it's missing and then aborts.

It often happens that when an error occurs, you want to print a message and abort. These functions are combined in the word ABORT" ("abort-quote"):

WORD	STACK	ACTION
ABORT"	f --	Compiled in the form: ABORT" ccc" If flag f is true, prints the message ccc and takes a system-dependent error action which includes ABORT.

The system-dependent error action can include automatically "forgetting" a defective definition or tracing the execution path leading to the error. In addition, many systems include a vectored (deferred) word in the error action. This lets you substitute error actions which are more suitable for the program at hand.

Here is a more readable definition of ['] using ABORT":

```
: '  ( -- addr)
\ returns the compilation address of the next
\ word in the input stream.
  BL WORD FIND  ( addr flag)
  0= ABORT" MISSING"  ;
```

CODE words

FORTH contains a built-in assembler for writing selected words directly in machine code. FORTH is inherently more portable than machine code in that it can run unchanged on different computers. Nevertheless, there are times you may wish to consider the extra speed of machine code.

Most programs spend roughly 80% of their time in 20% of their code. If you rewrite this 20% of a FORTH program as machine code, you might see a dramatic increase in the speed of execution. A good compromise between speed and portability is to first write your entire program in FORTH and then to replace selected words with machine code. This way, the original FORTH source code is available to you if you ever need to move your program to a different computer. You can keep the FORTH source code on screens near the machine-code source. You can even use conditional compilation to select between FORTH and machine-code versions of a program.

Machine-code words take this form:

```
CODE <name>
  ...
  machine-code instructions
  ...
  return sequence
END-CODE
```

The defining word CODE creates a dictionary entry of the given name. The word END-CODE (sometimes called [C;] "c-semicolon") ends the definition. A machine-code definition differs from a colon definition in several important respects:

- The code field of the header points to the body of the definition, where the machine code is assembled.

- The context is set to the ASSEMBLER vocabulary. The colon normally sets the context to current.
- The text interpreter remains in the interpret mode. Assembler opcodes and operands are interpreted and not compiled. Each opcode is responsible for adding the appropriate machine instruction to the end of the dictionary--thus the full power of FORTH is available for number and address computations.
- The machine code definition must end by assembling a jump instruction to the special address NEXT.

The format of the FORTH assembler differs greatly from machine to machine and differs between FORTHs as well. You should consult your FORTH system documentation for details.

The word ;CODE ("semicolon-code") is the machine-code equivalent of DOES>. Used inside a defining word, ;CODE sets the run-time action of any word subsequently defined by that defining word to a machine-code sequence:

```
: CONSTANT
  CREATE ,   ( n --)
  ;CODE      ( -- n)
    ...
    machine code for constant
    ...
    return sequence
  END-CODE

5 CONSTANT FIVE  OK
```

Any new constants will now run the machine code in CONSTANT--as in the following diagram:

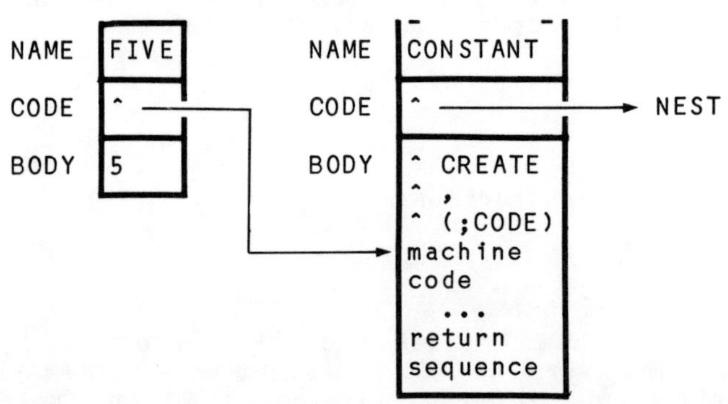

In many FORTHs, DOES> is implemented as a special form of ;CODE. The compiling word DOES> compiles both the (;CODE) and a machine-code call to the run-time code for DOES>, called (DOES>) or DODOES>. This run-time code has two actions:

1. It pushes the address of the body of the defined word on the stack.

2. It adjusts the instruction pointer so that the next FORTH word executed is the FORTH code that followed the DOES> in the defining word.
   The net effect is that the code field of the defined word appears to be redirected to point to the FORTH code that followed the DOES> in the defining word.

Here is a diagram of what happens when you create a VALUE:

```
: VALUE
  CREATE ,   ( n --)
  DOES> @ ;  ( -- n)

4 VALUE FOUR  OK
```

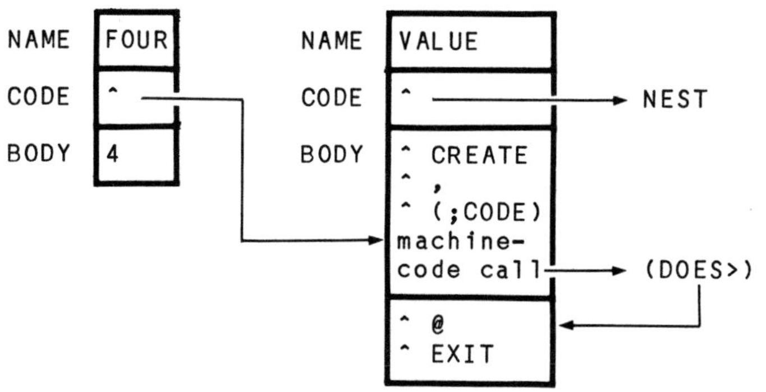

Bit manipulation

The logical operators AND, OR, and NOT presented in the chapter on flow of control are "bitwise" operators. This means they examine each pair of bits in the two operands independently. For example, suppose you OR two binary numbers together:

```
    0001001000110100  (hex 1234)
OR  1010101111001101  (hex ABCD)
    ----------------
    1011101111111101  (hex BBFD)
```

Each bit in the answer is simply the logical OR of the two bits above it.

What if you AND the numbers 2 and 4?

```
    0000000000000010  (2)
AND 0000000000000100  (4)
    ----------------
    0000000000000000  (0)
```

If you are using 2 and 4 as flags, you get the surprising result that TRUE AND TRUE is FALSE. To prevent situations like this, be sure that at least one of the flags is Boolean, since Boolean flags are either all zeroes (0) or all ones (-1).

You can use logical operators to manipulate bits within a number. They can

Set a bit (to one).
Reset a bit (to zero).
Detect whether a bit is set or not.
Reverse a bit.

To set a bit, you can OR it with a one in the appropriate position, and you can clear a bit by ANDing it with zero. Bits are usually numbered from right to left, starting with zero. If you wanted to set bit 3 of a number, you would OR it with binary 0000000000001000 (8):

```
    0101010101010101  (hex 5555)
 OR 0000000000001000  (hex 0008)
    ----------------
    0101010101011101  (hex 555D)
```

You could clear it again with a (hex) FFF7 AND:

```
    0101010101011101  (hex 555D)
AND 1111111111110111  (hex FFF7)
    ----------------
    0101010101011101  (hex 5555)
```

To see whether bit 3 is set, AND it with 0000000000001000 (8):

```
    ????????????????
AND 0000000000001000
    ----------------
    000000000000?000
```

If bit 3 is one, the result will be 8 (TRUE); otherwise it will be zero (FALSE). The other bits are ignored or "masked out."

Bits can be selectively reversed with the XOR ("x-or") exclusive-OR logical function. An exclusive-OR of two bits is one if either of the two bits (but not both) is one. In other words, if one of the two bits is set, the other will be reversed:

```
    1010101010101010  (hex AAAA)
XOR 1111111111111111  ( -1)
    ----------------
    0101010101010101  (hex 5555)
```

If all bits are reversed, as in the example above, you have the logical operation NOT:

```
: NOT  ( n -- not-n)  -1 XOR  ;
```

Bit manipulation is often used in situations where hardware has been "mapped" into main memory. Suppose the keyboard is mapped into hexadecimal address C000. This means that reading the value at address C000 is the same as reading the keyboard, so the sequence C000 C@ reads a key. Suppose further that bit 7 at this location is set by the hardware whenever a key is pressed:

```
address  value (at bit)

         7 6-through-0
 C000:  [?][ASCII code]
         |
         v
         0 = key not pressed.
         1 = key pressed.
```

You can use this definition of KEY? to see if a key is pressed:

```
: KEY?  ( -- f)
\ returns true if a key is pressed.
  C000 C@ 80 ( 10000000 mask) AND
  0<> ; ( convert to Boolean flag)
```

Byte manipulation

The low-order byte of a number can be found simply by ANDing it with the appropriate mask:

```
HEX ABCD  OK
00FF AND . CD  OK
```

The high-order byte can be found by "shifting" it into the low-order byte and then masking it as above. Shifting a number to the right one bit is equivalent to dividing it by two:

```
     1010101111001101  (hex ABCD)
     ----------------
2/   1101010111100110  (hex D5E6)
```

The signed operator 2/ keeps bit 15 set to one (negative). The previous bit 15 (and all other bits) move one place to the right. This is called "propagating the sign bit."

We can define operators to shift signed numbers to the right or the left any number of times:

```
: >SHIFT  ( n1 n2 -- n3)
\ shift n1 n2 bits to the right.
  0 ?DO  2/  LOOP  ;

: <SHIFT  ( n1 n2 -- n3)
\ shift n1 n2 bits to the left.
  0 ?DO  2*  LOOP  ;
```

When these shift operators are written in machine code, they run many times faster than the equivalent multiplication and division commands.

The high-order byte of a number can now be isolated this way:

```
HEX ABCD  OK
8 >SHIFT  00FF AND . AB  OK
```

A number can be simultaneously split into high- and low-order bytes with the word SPLIT:

```
: SPLIT  ( n -- low-n high-n)
\ splits n into low-order and high-order bytes.
  DUP 00FF AND  SWAP 8 >SHIFT 00FF AND  ;
```

The complementary function is COMBINE:

```
: COMBINE  ( n-low-byte n-high-byte -- n)
\ combines two numbers into one.  The high-order
\ bytes of the two numbers are ignored.
  SWAP 00FF AND  SWAP 8 <SHIFT  OR  ;

HEX ABCD  SPLIT . . AB CD  OK
CC34 CC12 COMBINE . 1234  OK
```

SPLIT and COMBINE together give you complete byte manipulation. You can use them to write the word FLIP, which interchanges the low- and high-order bytes in a number:

```
: FLIP  ( n1 -- n2)
\ interchanges the bytes of n1 to form n2.
  SPLIT SWAP COMBINE  ;

HEX 4321 FLIP . 2143  OK
```

The random-number generator we used earlier in the book can be improved with FLIP.

```
: RANDOM  ( n -- random-number)
  RAND FLIP  SWAP MOD  ;
```

This works better because the high-order byte of the number returned by RAND is more random than the low-order byte.

One final word

We have introduced you to all of the words required by the Forth-83 Standard except one:

```
FORTH-83  OK
```

This word guarantees that a Forth-83 Standard system is available. This is assured by making it the last definition in the system dictionary--if FORTH-83 is in the dictionary, then all other standard words are, too.

WORD	STACK	ACTION
CODE name	--	Begins a machine-code definition by creating a dictionary entry for <name> and activating the built-in assembler.
END-CODE	--	Ends a machine-code definition.
;CODE	--	The machine-code equivalent for DOES>. Redirects the code field of later definitions to the machine code that follows it in the body of the defining word. See the text for details.
ASSEMBLER	--	The assembler vocabulary.
XOR	n1 n2 -- n3	Returns the exclusive-OR of n1 and n2.
FORTH-83	--	Guarantees that a Forth-83 Standard system is available and ready.

Exercises

1. Redefine / to protect against division by zero:

```
10 0 / ZERO-DIVIDE
```

Redefine DUP to prevent it from working on an empty stack:

```
CLEAR DUP EMPTY-STACK
```

Put these new definitions into a new vocabulary called SAFETY. When you use SAFETY, you'll be using safer (but slower) versions of these words.

2. Using the bitwise logical operators, define the functions CSET, CRESET, and CTOGGLE. These words use an 8-bit mask to set, reset, and reverse (toggle) selected bits at an address. Their syntax is as follows:

```
CSET    ( mask addr --) \ sets bits at addr.
CRESET  ( mask addr --) \ resets bits at addr.
CTOGGLE ( mask addr --) \ reverses bits at addr.
```

3. The exclusive-OR function XOR is often used in cryptography. Write a word XCODE to encode a string by exclusive-ORing the value of each character with its address. Using XCODE again decodes the string, provided that it's at the same address. XCODE in action should look something like this:

```
20 STRING SALUTE  OK
" HAVE A NICE DAY." SALUTE S!  OK

SALUTE XCODE  OK
SALUTE TYPE ADF123418DSJVDLX  OK

SALUTE XCODE  OK
SALUTE TYPE HAVE A NICE DAY.  OK
```

For advanced students:

4. Study the documentation for the built-in assembler in your FORTH. See if you can write the CODE versions of the shift operators <SHIFT and >SHIFT.

Solutions to problems

Chapter 2

```
1.  : BLIP  CR INSET STAR ;

    : T  ROW BLIP BLIP BLIP BLIP ;

    : I  ROW BLIP BLIP BLIP ROW ;
    : C  ROW CR STAR CR STAR CR STAR ROW ;
    : E  ROW CR STAR ROW      CR STAR ROW ;

2.  : BOOP  CR ." *   *" ;

    : H  BOOP BOOP ROW BOOP BOOP ;
    : U  BOOP BOOP BOOP BOOP ROW ;

3.  : HI-TECH   H I CR ROW CR T E C H ;
```

Chapter 3

```
1.  : TRIANGLE  CR ." THE AREA IS "  * 2/ . ;

2.  : CENTIGRADE>FAHRENHEIT  9 * 5 / 32 + ;
    : FAHRENHEIT>CENTIGRADE  32 - 5 * 9 / ;

3.  : CHANGE  0 ;
    : QUARTERS  25 * + ;
    : DIMES     10 * + ;
    : NICKELS    5 * + ;
    : PENNIES        + ;
    : FRANCS    27 * + ;
    : KRONOR    13 * + ;
    : MARKS     40 * + ;
    : TOKENS    75 * + ;
```

```
: INTO
  25 /MOD CR . ." QUARTERS"
  10 /MOD CR . ." DIMES"
  5  /MOD CR . ." NICKELS"
          CR . ." PENNIES" ;
```

Chapter 4

```
1.  : 3DUP  2 PICK 2 PICK 2 PICK ;
    : NIP   SWAP DROP ;
    : TUCK  SWAP OVER ;

    : 3DUP  DUP 2OVER ROT ;

2.  : RECTANGLE
      ROT - -ROT  SWAP - *
      CR ." THE AREA IS " . ;
```

```
SCR # 5
\ Chapter 5 Answers
( Problem 1)
: BLIP  ( --)
\ a block-letter stem primitive.
  CR INSET STAR ;

\ Some block-letters:
: T  ( --)  ROW BLIP BLIP BLIP BLIP ;

: I  ( --)  ROW BLIP BLIP BLIP ROW ;
: C  ( --)  ROW CR STAR CR STAR CR STAR ROW ;
: E  ( --)  ROW CR STAR ROW     CR STAR ROW ;
```

```
SCR # 6
\ Chapter 5 Answers (continued)
( Problem 2)
: BOOP
\ another block-letter primitive.
  CR ." *   *" ;

\ Some block-letters:
: H  ( -- )  BOOP BOOP ROW BOOP BOOP ;
: U  ( -- )  BOOP BOOP BOOP BOOP ROW ;

( Problem 3)
: HI-TECH
\ prints a giant message.
  H I CR ROW CR T E C H ;


SCR # 7
\ Chapter 6 Answers
( Problem 1)
: OFF  ( addr --)
\ sets the value at addr to FALSE (0).
  0  SWAP !  ;

: ON   ( addr --)
\ sets the value at addr to TRUE (-1).
  -1 SWAP !  ;

( Problem 2)
: VARIABLE  ( n --)  ( -- addr)
\ creates a FIG-style variable with initial value n.
  CREATE  ,  ;


SCR # 8
\ Chapter 6 Answers (continued)
( Problem 3)
CREATE STACK  ( extra stack)
  32 ALLOT    ( 32 bytes = 16 cells)

VARIABLE STACK-INDEX  ( next stack position index)
 STACK-INDEX OFF      ( 0 STACK-INDEX !)

\ Push and pop from extra stack:
: PUSH  ( n --)
  STACK STACK-INDEX @ + !
  STACK-INDEX @ 2+ 30 MIN STACK-INDEX !  ;

: POP   ( -- n)
  STACK-INDEX @ 2- 0 MAX DUP STACK-INDEX !
  STACK + @  ;
```

```
SCR # 9
\ Chapter 7 Answers
( Problem 1)
: MAX  ( n1 n2 -- n3)  2DUP < IF SWAP THEN DROP ;
: MIN  ( n1 n2 -- n3)  2DUP > IF SWAP THEN DROP ;

( Problem 2)
: 0>   ( n1 -- flag)  NEGATE 0<  ;
: 0<>  ( n1 -- flag)  0= NOT  ;

( Problem 3)
: NAND  ( n1 n2 -- n3)  AND NOT  ;
```

```
SCR # 10
\ Chapter 7 Answers (continued)
( Problem 4)
: NOT   TRUE NAND  ;
: AND   NAND NOT  ;
: OR    NOT SWAP NOT NAND  ;

: XOR  ( n1 n2 -- n3)
  2DUP NOT AND  -ROT SWAP NOT AND  OR  ;
```

```
SCR # 11
\ Chapter 7 Answers (continued)
( Problem 5)
CREATE DAYS/MONTH
 00 C, ( January is month #1)
 31 C, 28 C, 31 C, 30 C, 31 C, 30 C,
 31 C, 31 C, 30 C, 31 C, 30 C, 31 C,

VARIABLE MONTH
VARIABLE YEAR

: DAYS  ( -- n)
\ computes the # of days in MONTH for YEAR.
  DAYS/MONTH MONTH @ + C@
  MONTH @ 2 = YEAR @ 4 MOD 0= AND  ( leap year?)
  IF  1+  THEN  ;
```

```
SCR # 12
\ Chapter 7 Answers (continued)
( Problem 6)
VARIABLE SECRET#     ( the secret number)
VARIABLE OLD-ERROR   ( the prior guess error)
VARIABLE #GUESSES    ( the number of incorrect guesses)

: GAME   ( --)
\ sets up the secret number.
   100 RANDOM 1+  DUP SECRET# !
   0 #GUESSES !  101 OLD-ERROR ! ;

: YOU-WIN!   ( --)
\ prints winning message.
   CR  ." YOU WON IN "  #GUESSES @ .  ." GUESSES! "  ;
```

```
SCR # 13
\ Chapter 7 Answers (continued)
( Problem 6)
: GUESS   ( guess --)
\ plays "Guess the number."
   1 #GUESSES +!
   DUP SECRET# @ =            IF  YOU-WIN!  ELSE
   DUP SECRET# @ - ABS 3  < IF  ." HOT!"  ELSE
   ( compute error size:)
       SECRET# @ - ABS  OLD-ERROR @  OVER OLD-ERROR !
   ( new-error old-error) < IF  ." WARMER"  ELSE  ." COLDER"
   THEN THEN THEN  ;
```

```
SCR # 14
\ Chapter 8 Answers
( Problem 1)
CREATE BOXES  ( creates and initialize box array:)
 3 , 2 , 0 , 4 , 0 , 1 , 4 , 2 , 2 , 3 ,

: BOX?  ( size --)
\ selects a box, deleting it from BOXES.
   9 MIN ( sizes 0-9)  FALSE  ( assume no boxes)
   10 ROT ( check same or larger sizes)
   DO  DROP  BOXES I 2* + @  ?DUP  ( any boxes?)
      IF  I .  1- BOXES I 2* + !  TRUE LEAVE  THEN
      FALSE
   LOOP  0= IF  ." NO BOXES"  THEN  ;
```

```
SCR # 15
\ Chapter 8 Answers (continued)
( Problem 2)
: STARS  ( n --)
\ prints n stars.
  0 ?DO  ." *" ( STAR)  LOOP  ;

( Problem 3)
: BOUNDS  ( addr length -- limit initial)
\ converts address and length into DO ... LOOP form.
  OVER + SWAP  ;

( Problem 4)
: HISTOGRAM  ( addr length --)
\ displays array of cells as histogram.
  2* BOUNDS  DO  CR I @ STARS  2 +LOOP  ;

```

```
SCR # 16
\ Chapter 9 Answers
( Problem 1)
: GROWTH?  ( percent --)
\ finds how long it takes 1000 to double at this percent.
  >R  0 ( count) 1000
  BEGIN  1 0 D+  ( increment count)
    DUP R@ 100 */ +  DUP 1999 >
  UNTIL  R> 2DROP .  ;

( Problem 2)
: CONE  ( r=radius h=height -- area)
  OVER * *  355 339 ( PI/3) */  ;

( Problem 3)
: D>S  ( d -- s)  DROP  ;

```

```
SCR # 17
\ Chapter 9 Answers (continued)
( Problem 4)
VARIABLE FUDGE  ( double-number fudge factor)

: D1~  ( d1 d2 -- f)
\ true if d1 = d2 within fudge factor.
  D- DABS D>S  FUDGE @ > NOT  ;

( Problem 5)
: .S  ( --)
  ?STACK  CR ." STACK: "  DEPTH ?DUP
  IF  0
    DO  DEPTH I - 1- PICK  BASE @ 10 = IF . ELSE U. THEN
    LOOP
  ELSE ." EMPTY"
  THEN  ;
```

```
SCR # 18
\ Chapter 10 Answers
( Problem 1)
: <CMOVE>   ( addr1 addr2 n --)
\ safely moves n overlapping bytes from addr1 to addr2.
  >R  2DUP U< NOT  IF R> CMOVE  ELSE R> CMOVE> THEN  ;

( Problem 2)
VARIABLE KEY-DELAY

: WAIT-KEY  ( -- key)
\ waits for key to be pressed, then reads it.
  BEGIN  KEY? NOT WHILE  1 KEY-DELAY +!  REPEAT  KEY  ;
```

```
SCR # 19
\ Chapter 10 Answers (continued)
( Problem 3)
: UPPER  ( string -- string')
\ converts a string to upper case.
  2DUP BOUNDS
  ?DO  I C@ DUP ASCII a < SWAP ASCII z > OR NOT
       IF  I C@ BL - I C!  THEN
  LOOP  ;
```

```
SCR # 20
\ Chapter 10 Answers (continued)
( Problem 4)
VARIABLE DPL

: NUMBER  ( string -- dn)
\ converts string to number.
\ Saves decimal location in DPL.
  -1 DPL !  ( assume no decimal)
  PAD SWAP CPACK  BL PAD COUNT + C!
  0 0       ( double accumulator)
  PAD 1+ C@ ASCII - = DUP >R -    ( handle minus sign)
  PAD CONVERT  DUP C@ ASCII . =  ( handle decimal point)
  IF DUP >R CONVERT  DUP R> - 1- DPL ! THEN
  DROP R> IF DNEGATE THEN  ;
```

```
SCR # 21
\ Chapter 10 Answers (continued)
( Problem 5)
: SCAN ( string delimiter -- string')
\ returns shortened string from first string position
\ equal to delimiter.  If string is empty or contains
\ no delimiters, a length of zero is returned.
  >R 2DUP BOUNDS
  ?DO  I C@ R@ = IF LEAVE THEN  1 /STRING  LOOP
  R> DROP  ;

: LEX  ( string delimiter -- left-string right-string)
\ split string in two at delimiter.
  >R 2DUP R>  SCAN
  ROT OVER - -ROT
  DUP 0<> NEGATE /STRING  ;
```

```
SCR # 22
\ Chapter 10 Answers (continued)
( Problem 6)
: D.  ( d --)
\ prints double number with commas.
  <#
  BEGIN  # 2DUP D0= NOT
    IF   # 2DUP D0= NOT
    IF   # THEN THEN
           2DUP D0= NOT
  WHILE  ASCII , HOLD
  REPEAT #>  TYPE SPACE  ;
```

```
SCR # 23
\ Chapter 10 Answers (continued)
( Problem 7)
: IN   ( string1 string2 -- offset true)
       ( string1 string2 -- 0)
\ returns the position of string1 in string2.
\ Offset is zero if string1 is found in 1st position.
  DUP 3 PICK - DUP 0<  ( match impossible?)
  IF  DROP 2DROP 2DROP FALSE EXIT  THEN
  0 ( count) FALSE ( match?) ROT 1+ 0
  DO  DROP >R
    2OVER 2OVER DROP OVER COMPARE 0= ( equal?)
    IF  R> TRUE LEAVE  THEN
    1 /STRING  R> 1+ FALSE
  LOOP
  >R >R  2SWAP 2DROP 2SWAP 2DROP  R> R>
  DUP 0= IF  NIP  THEN  ;
```

```
SCR # 24
\ Chapter 11 Answers
( Problem 1)
: STRING
\ creates a string variable with a stored max-length.
  CREATE  ( size --)
    0 MAX 255 MIN  DUP C, 0 C,  ALLOT
  DOES>  ( -- string)  1+ COUNT  ;

( Problem 2)
: COUNTER  ( --)  \ create counter.
  CREATE  0 ,  DOES>  1 SWAP +!  ;

: RESET    ( --)  \ resets counter.
  ' >BODY  0 SWAP !  ( OFF)  ;
: EXAMINE  ( --)  \ prints counter.
  ' >BODY  @ .      ( ?)     ;

SCR # 25
\ Chapter 11 Answers (continued)
( Problem 3)
: 2VALUE  \ double-number value.
  CREATE  ( d --)  , ,  DOES>  ( -- d)  2@  ;

( Problem 4)
VARIABLE COLOR-REGISTER

: COLOR   \ create a color register.
  CREATE  ( n --)  ,
  DOES>  ( --)  @ COLOR-REGISTER !  ;

SCR # 26
\ Chapter 11 Answers (continued)
( Problem 5)
VARIABLE SCALE

: POINT   \ creates a scaled point.
  CREATE  ( x y --)  SWAP , ,
  DOES>  ( -- x' y')  2@ SCALE @ TUCK * -ROT *  ;
```

```
SCR # 27
\ Chapter 12 Answers
( Problem 1)
: DLITERAL  ( d --) ( -- d)
  SWAP [COMPILE] LITERAL [COMPILE] LITERAL  ;
 IMMEDIATE

( Problem 2)
: ?LEAVE  ( --)
  [COMPILE] IF [COMPILE] LEAVE [COMPILE] THEN  ;
 IMMEDIATE

( Problem 3)
: (SELECT)  ( n --)
\ run-time for SELECT.  Assumes pre-increment.
  1+ ( skip address) 2* R@ + @ EXECUTE
  R> @ >R  ;

SCR # 28
\ Chapter 12 Answers (continued)
( Problem 3 continued)
: SELECT  ( --) ( n --)
\ performs the nth action that follows; skips others.
\ The address to skip to is resolved by COMPLETE.
  COMPILE (SELECT)  >MARK  ;  IMMEDIATE

: COMPLETE  ( --)
\ ends a SELECT--COMPLETE structure.
  >RESOLVE  ;  IMMEDIATE

( Problem 4)
: BODY-OF  ( -- pfa)
  STATE @  IF  [COMPILE] ['] COMPILE >BODY
           ELSE  ' >BODY
           THEN  ;  IMMEDIATE

SCR # 29
\ Chapter 13 Answers
( Problem 1)
: CONTROL  ( -- n)
\ used in the form: CONTROL c
\ where c follows in the input stream.
\ returns the ASCII control code of c.
  BL WORD 1+ C@  ASCII @ -
  STATE @  IF  [COMPILE] LITERAL  THEN  ;
 IMMEDIATE
```

```
SCR # 30
\ Chapter 13 Answers (continued)
( Problem 2)
: SEARCH  ( string n1 n2 --)
\ searches screens n1 thru n2 for string match.
  1+ SWAP       ( each block)
  ?DO   16 0   ( each line)
     DO  2DUP J BLOCK I 64 * + 64 IN  ( match?)
       IF  DROP CR J . I .           ( type line)
                J BLOCK I 64 * + 64 TYPE
       THEN
     LOOP
  LOOP  2DROP  ;
```

```
SCR # 31
\ Chapter 13 Answers (continued)
( Problem 3)
  4 CONSTANT FIRST-BLOCK
100 CONSTANT RECORD-SIZE

: RECORD  ( record# buffer-addr --)
\ reads virtual record into buffer.
  SWAP RECORD-SIZE *
  1024 /MOD FIRST-BLOCK + SWAP
  1024 OVER - >R  RECORD-SIZE R@ -  0>
  IF   OVER 1+ BLOCK  3 PICK
       RECORD-SIZE R@ /STRING  CMOVE
  THEN SWAP BLOCK +  SWAP
       RECORD-SIZE R> MIN      CMOVE  ;
```

```
SCR # 32
\ Chapter 13 Answers (continued)
( Problem 4)  34 LOAD
 0 FIELD NAME  ( 20-byte)  20 FIELD STREET  ( 30-byte)
50 FIELD CITY  ( 20-byte)  70 FIELD STATE   ( 3-byte)
73 FIELD ZIP   ( 4-byte)

CREATE BUF  9 ALLOT  35 LOAD

: FILE-IT  ( --)
  SELECT-IT  ( choose a record)
  CR ."   NAME:"   NAME 19 READ-IT
  CR ." STREET:" STREET 29 READ-IT
  CR ."   CITY:"   CITY 19 READ-IT
  CR ."  STATE:"  STATE  2 READ-IT
  CR ."    ZIP:"  BUF 9 EXPECT
  BUF SPAN @ VAL  DROP ZIP 2!  ;
```

```
SCR # 33
\ Chapter 13 Answers (continued)
( Problem 4 continued)
: PRINT-IT  ( --)
  SELECT-IT  ( choose a record)
  CR ."   NAME:"   NAME COUNT TYPE
  CR ." STREET:" STREET COUNT TYPE
  CR ."   CITY:"   CITY COUNT TYPE
  CR ."  STATE:"  STATE COUNT TYPE
  CR ."    ZIP:"    ZIP 2@ D.  ;
```

```
SCR # 34
\ Chapter 13 Answers (continued)
( Problem 5)
: "   ( --) ( -- string)
\ compiles a string or leaves it on the stack.
\ Uses the word (") described in the text.
\ For NIP and TUCK see chapter 4 exercises.
  PAD OFF  SOURCE NIP >R
  BEGIN
    ASCII " PARSE  R@ >IN @ = DUP 0=
    IF DROP  2DUP + 1+ C@ ASCII " = DUP >R
       NEGATE DUP >IN +! +  R> 0=
    THEN  -ROT
    TUCK  PAD COUNT + SWAP CMOVE  PAD C@ + PAD C!
  UNTIL  R> DROP  PAD COUNT  STATE @ ( compiling?)
  IF COMPILE (")  HERE OVER 1+ ALLOT  SWAP CPACK
  THEN  ;  IMMEDIATE
```

```
SCR # 35
\ Chapter 14 Answers
( Problem 1)
VOCABULARY SAFETY
ONLY FORTH ALSO  SAFETY DEFINITIONS

: /   ( n1 n2 -- n3)  DUP 0= ABORT" ZERO-DIVIDE" ;
: DUP   ( n -- n n)  DEPTH 0> NOT ABORT" EMPTY-STACK" ;

ONLY FORTH DEFINITIONS ALSO

( Problem 2)
\ sets, resets, or toggles byte at address.
: CSET      ( mask addr --)  TUCK C@ OR       SWAP C! ;
: CTOGGLE   ( mask addr --)  TUCK C@ XOR      SWAP C! ;
: CRESET    ( mask addr --)  TUCK C@
  SWAP NOT AND SWAP C! ;
```

```
SCR # 36
\ Chapter 14 Answers (continued)
( Problem 3)
: XCODE  ( string --)
\ encodes/decodes string in place.
  BOUNDS  ?DO  I C@ I XOR I C!  LOOP  ;
```

Index to FORTH words

The Forth-83 Standard word set is presented here in ASCII order. Each word is followed by an attribute list, the page number of the table in which it appears, and the page numbers where it is described in the text. The attributes listed are

I - IMMEDIATE
C - compile-only.

An index of supplementary words (defined in the text and not part of the Forth-83 Standard) immediately follows.

Forth-83 required word set

Double-number extension word set

Assembler extension word set

System extension word set

Search order specification and control

Definition field address conversion operators

Supplementary words

Supplementary string extension words

Index